Other books by Patricia Taylor Wells

The Eyes of the Doe

Mademoiselle Renoir à Paris

Lodestar

The Sand Rose

Kaleidoscope

I0155010

MAPLE POINT

KEUKA LAKE, NEW YORK

Patricia Taylor Wells

Bink Books
Bedazzled Ink Publishing Company • Fairfield, California

© 2024 Patricia Taylor Wells

All rights reserved. No part of this publication may be reproduced
or transmitted in any means,
electronic or mechanical, without permission in
writing from the publisher.

978-1-949290-95-0 paperback

Cover Design
by

Sapling
Studio

Bink Books
a division of
Bedazzled Ink Publishing Company
Fairfield, California
http://www.bedazzledink.com

In Memory of Barbara Bush Wells
1918 – 2009

Acknowledgments

This book would not have been possible without the help of my husband, Robert Bush Wells, who provided a wealth of background information on the events and people associated with Maple Point. The time he spent at the cottage during his childhood was influenced by his Great Uncle Bob and Great Aunt Ada, who established traditions that would long be cherished and observed.

I am also grateful for the help and information I received from Barbara Bush Walter, the daughter of Robert Sayre Bush and the niece of Barbara Bush Wells. My appreciation also goes to my brother and sister-in-law, Lee III and Alicia Wells, for their contribution to this work and their support and encouragement.

Keuka Lake

The best place on Earth I've ever been to is Maple Point, the nineteenth-century cottage passed down to and owned by my husband's mother until she sold it in 2005. I thought it was a town or village rather than a home when I first heard about it. But after spending twenty-two years each summer at this iconic location, I realized it was not just a place, but a way of life, that became my sanctuary then and now.

Maple Point lies halfway between Hammondsport and Penn Yan in upstate New York on East Bluff Drive overlooking Keuka Lake's deep, clear, sparkling waters. Keuka stretches across west-central New York and is the third largest of the Finger Lakes. Altogether, eleven of these long, narrow lakes make up this region, which, on a map, resemble the fingers of an outstretched hand.

A legend attributed to the Iroquois Native Americans who inhabited the Finger Lakes region as early as 1000 CE tells how the Great Spirit reached down and pressed his hands against the earth one day to bless it. The imprint of his fingers left behind eleven lakes altogether due to the Great Spirit having an extra finger shaped like a two-pronged fork, which is why, according to legend, Keuka Lake is Y-shaped and has two branches.

Archeologists, however, estimate that the lakes were created long before the legend. Millions of years ago, there were no lakes, only streams flowing northward through V-shaped valleys. During the Pleistocene Ice Age, which began about 2.5 million years ago, these valleys were buried under large ice sheets. For thousands of years, the glaciers advanced southward from Canada. As the earth warmed, the ice receded. The melted water flowed into the deep trenches that the glaciers had chiseled on the bottoms and sides of the valleys, transforming them into the beautiful Finger Lakes.

There is some evidence of pre-Iroquois inhabitants on Keuka's Bluff Point. The only thing that remains is the ruins of these mysterious structures, which some speculate were built by Nordic visitors before Columbus set sail for the New World. The Seneca Indians tell of "a great canoe, manned by men with flowing hair, and carrying shining shields on its side." There are several conflicting accounts of who may have settled briefly in this region and the purpose for the structures they left behind. No one disagrees, however, that Keuka Lake was and still is a favorite fishing site.

The five members of the Iroquois Confederacy or League, which include the Cayuga, Onondaga, Seneca, Oneida, and Mohawk tribes, are referred to as the *Haudenosaunee* or people of the long house. They are called this because they live in long houses made of elm bark that house several families, often as many as twenty. During the winter, they gather inside these elongated structures to tell stories, perform ceremonies, or socialize.

The two largest lakes, Seneca and Cayuga, were named after Iroquois League nations. The names of the other lakes were based on characteristics or surroundings. Keuka means "canoe landing" in the Iroquois language and is translated as "lake with an elbow" in the Seneca language. Early European settlers called Keuka Lake "Crooked Lake" because of its unique Y shape. Even today, merchants still use this moniker with their business name.

Of all the lakes, Keuka stands out for several reasons. It is positioned in the middle of the eleven Finger Lakes like a fork in the road. Keuka is the only lake in the country that flows north and south because of its two branches. It flows north from Hammondsport to Penn Yan up the East Branch and south from Branchport to the end of the Bluff down the West Branch. It then combines with the water flowing north from the lake's southern end. Keuka empties into Seneca Lake, while the other Finger Lakes drain north into rivers that eventually wind their way to Lake Ontario.

Keuka is 19.6 miles long and 1.9 miles wide at its broadest point. It is 715 feet above sea level and has a maximum depth of 187 feet, which is shallower than its sister lakes. The Bluff, which straddles the East and West Branches, is 1,426 feet above sea level at its highest point.

This "Lady of the Lakes," as it is sometimes called, is often deemed the most beautiful of the Finger Lakes. Most of the shoreline is dotted with residential dwellings, but several locations have public access to the lake. The lake is a favorite for fishing, boating, and swimming. Many families own lake homes passed down from generation to generation, and even those who don't own property often vacation on Keuka Lake every year. It's that kind of place. Once you've experienced Keuka Lake's natural beauty and serenity, you keep coming back.

The Holmes Steamboat Docked at Maple Point Landing on Keuka Lake, July 1899 (Photo from Gleason/Bush/Wells Collection)

Several notable vineyards and wineries have sprung up over the years in the Keuka Lake area due to a favorable climate and soil conditions similar to the Champagne region in France. The first bonded winery, Pleasant Valley Wine Company, was established in 1860. The Finger Lake wineries attract visitors worldwide and are considered some of the top wine producers in the United States. Keuka stands out among them as having the lengthiest history of winemaking, dating back to 1829 when grapes were first grown along its shores near Hammondsport.

From 1835 to 1922, steamboats ferried back and forth on Keuka Lake. They mainly carried grapes and other freight to nearby railroads, cities, and wineries. Later, passengers used steamers to get where they were going quicker and easier. There were several landings, and one of them was Maple Point. By 1895, there were a total of seven steamboats on Keuka Lake.

On the northeastern tip of the lake, Penn Yan, named after its Pennsylvania and Yankee settlers, makes up one of the three villages on the lakeshore. Branchport is on the northwestern end of Keuka, and it was initially known as "Esperanza." Later, its name was changed in keeping with its north branch location. Hammondsport, which lies on the south end of the lake, was named after its founder, Lazarus Hammond.

Keuka Lake is an idyllic location rich in history, natural beauty, and unimaginable tranquility. And though I no longer lie in the porch hammock on a warm summer day, watching boats glide across its sun-glistened waters with sails like the folded wings of butterflies, I often go there in my thoughts. And once more, I relive the dream I had lived for many years.

Sail Boats

I would lie in the hammock on summer days;
The sky's blue reflected on the lake,
A soft breeze would tumble over the hillside
And parachute into the valley.
The dog would jump up on my lap and muzzle
The open book spread across my chest.
Soon, my eye travels to a panoramic scene
Of sailboats gliding in gentle daze
As the wind lifts and billows their canvases.
They moved as if they were graceful swans
And then disappeared as they rounded the bluff.
I closed my eyes and daydreamed awhile,
As the waves lapped against the dock house pilings
Like a thirsty dog slurping water.
Not long after, the sailboats came back around—
This time, turning in my direction.
When closer by, I squinted my eyes and watched
While crewmembers adjusted the sails,
That now seem like folded wings of butterflies
Waiting patiently to catch the wind.

Patricia Taylor Wells

Maple Point

Maple Point was described as one of the most handsome spots on Keuka's East Branch in *The Elmira Daily Advertiser* on July 26, 1902. The article went on to say, "The cottage itself is a marvel of beauty, and the boat landing is covered by a neat pavilion, which makes it the handsomest dock on the lake." According to Yates County property records, the home was built circa 1850. It was formerly the summer home of George Lapham, a merchant and the principal owner of First National Bank of Penn Yan. Later on, according to the *Penn Yan Democrat*, he was indicted by the United States Supreme Court for embezzlement due to his role as the bank's president when it failed in 1899. Mr. Lapham was never found guilty of the charges held against him.

In December 1892, Homer O. Brooks, the nephew of Rachel Brooks and her husband Silas O. Gleason, loaned thirty-eight hundred dollars to Steven B. and Harriet B. Ayres. Steven was the editor of the *Yates County Chronicle* and later a one-term U.S. Congressman. Half the loan amount was secured by a mortgage against their lake property, Maple Point. The mortgage was to be paid in full, along with interest, by the end of three years. In January 1893, just one month after loaning the money to the Ayres, Homer assigned the mortgage to his Uncle Silas.

In 1895, the mortgage was in arrears. Following a foreclosure lawsuit begun by Silas Gleason, Maple Point

Maple tree growing through Maple Point's porch roof, Circa 1899.
(Gleason/Bush/Wells Collection)

was sold at public auction to his son Edward for thirteen hundred dollars. Edward also paid a grand sum of thirty-five dollars for the contents of Maple Point, which were also sold at public auction. From then on, the story told by family members was that the cottage was acquired in payment for a debt owed to the Gleasons.

Maple Point was named for the large maple tree built around the cottage's front porch. A hole in the porch roof enabled the tree to grow through the ceiling for many years. The original building was a fishing shack. Later, the cottage was built in front of it, and the fishing shack became the kitchen and back entry. When the Gleasons took over the property, it had only two bedrooms. Later, the downstairs bedroom, which had a door to the outside, was added. Edward also built a boathouse in 1897. Edward's daughter Ada and her husband Bob had a full-time cook who slept in the downstairs bedroom once the cottage was passed on to them. In addition, Ada and Bob added an office, bathroom, and rear bedroom upstairs. They also remodeled the downstairs by moving the stairway to what used to be part of the side porch and adding a downstairs bath and two closets.

The large front porch was embroidered with gingerbread trim like the gazebo on the point and looked out over the lake. It was the gathering spot for family and friends who often challenged one another to a board game or zig-saw puzzle. The rocking chairs had a flexible ladder back with steel banding that ran through the slots on both sides of each horizontal slat. Today, the rocking chairs are on my back porch and are still in excellent condition. We have enjoyed their flexible backs and have only had to repaint them over the years.

The croquet court was below on the ground, and in the middle of the point was a tall flag pole made from the wooden mast and boom of a sailboat that had been spliced together. It was bolted to a six-by-six post buried in the ground and was taken down and stored every winter until the following season. The United States flag, a forty-eight-star version purchased at Pinckney Hardware in Penn Yan, was ceremoniously raised each morning and lowered every evening.

A Dutch windmill next to the flag pole was perched on a wooden platform attached to a staff. Behind the windmill was a sailboat. When a breeze blew, the sails would pivot back and forth, causing the platform to turn so that the windmill was facing the direction of the wind. There are photographs of the windmill dating back to 1935, but no one knows when it was first erected. One of the projects expected of visiting family members was painting the windmill's weathered features when needed.

Visitors could use the ornate cast iron rope pull doorbell on the porch to enter a large family/dining room. There was a brick fireplace in the corner with a wooden mantel. But what most people noticed was the intricate one-by-three beadboard tongue and groove paneling that alternated between oak and fir on both the walls and ceiling. The wainscoting had vertical boards, while the walls featured horizontal and forty-five-degree angled panels. The coffered ceiling offered interesting patterns of diagonal and straight-lay design. Fishing rods were hung above the wainscoting on the wall facing the porch. The upper section of the windows closest to the door opening onto the veranda was adorned with ruby red stained-glass squares in each corner. Across from the windows was a drop leaf table behind the living room sofa, and on it was a guest book.

 The kitchen had its challenges. Despite being large, there were no countertops, only tall cupboards that lined one wall. Initially, there was a cast iron wood stove that was used for cooking until an electric oven and stovetop were installed. For many years, the wood stove continued to provide heat on chilly days and was used to burn paper trash.

On another wall in the kitchen was a China cabinet with upper doors and glass windows made by Uncle Bob, who worked for a cabinet maker company.

Early on, there was a hand pump by the kitchen sink which was later replaced once the plumbing was upgraded with an electric pump motor for the water well.

The survey reference point for all properties near Maple Point was a tree outside the kitchen window. Once the stone patio below the kitchen steps was built, the survey reference was etched into the stone.

For many years, Aunt Ada and Uncle Bob set traditions that would last as long as the cottage remained in the Gleason, Bush, and Wells families. Aunt Ada was often referred to as the Queen Bee who oversaw every detail of life at Maple Point.

In 1983, I married Robert Bush Wells. I spent my summer vacations at the family cottage on Keuka Lake for the next twenty-two years. There has never been another place like it.

The Cottage

I knew who I was at the cottage,
I didn't think about the things I think about now.
I never wondered if I was loved or not,
Or if life had any purpose outside her rustic walls.
I simply knew who I was, and that was all that mattered.

It was my sanctuary, then and now—
The only place I ever belonged:
The floors, dappled by light passing through stained glass,
And the sound of waves lapping against the shore
Could heal any heart that was shattered.

And though I no longer lie in the hammock
Watching boats sail past on a warm summer day,
I sometimes go there in my thoughts—
And I feel like I'm finally home,
And my world is a little less tattered.

Patricia Taylor Wells

Rachel Brooks Gleason

The first woman doctor in the United States was Englishwoman Elizabeth Blackwell. In 1847, when she applied at Geneva Medical College in Ontario County in New York, the faculty allowed the student body to vote on her acceptance. The male students considered her application a joke, so they laughingly voted in her favor. Despite the discrimination that Blackwell faced during her study of Medicine, she graduated first in her class in 1849.

The same year that Elizabeth received her medical diploma, three more women were accepted at The Central Medical College in Syracuse, New York. The women were Sarah Adamson, Lydia Fowler, and Rachel B. Gleason. All three graduated in 1851, just minutes apart. Since their diplomas were awarded alphabetically, Rachel became the third American woman doctor but the fourth woman in the U.S. to earn her medical degree.

Rachel Ingall Brooks was born in 1820 in Winhall, far up in the hills of Vermont. Before the American Revolution, her family's homestead was founded as a wayside inn on the King's highway. When news that the Declaration of Independence had been proclaimed, the landlord filled everyone's cup to celebrate. A few years later, the inn became the beautiful home of Rachel's parents, Reuben M. Brooks and Lucy Muzzy Brooks. Rachel's mother gave birth to eight children, four of which died in infancy or early childhood.

When she turned eighteen, Rachel asked for permission to teach at a district school believed to have been in Rutland County. The district gladly accepted her services and arranged for her to board with a family near the little red schoolhouse where she taught. Initially, Rachel met with opposition from those who doubted her ability to control students who were more used to receiving discipline than learning. But the young woman who taught by choice rather than necessity surprised them all. One of her former students sent word twenty years later that her teaching had made his life successful. Rachel inspired her pupils through the love of knowledge she had acquired and sought as a young girl and with her patience, encouragement, and devotion to helping them learn. In the evenings, she would gather her students around her, with the youngest sitting on her lap as she read them stories.

It wasn't just the children Miss Brooks taught that admired her. According to someone related to the family with whom Rachel boarded, a tall, slender young man occasionally visited the school and its remarkable young teacher. Silas Gleason was a student at Castleton Medical College in Vermont. Although born in Massachusetts in 1818, his family moved to Vermont in 1823. After attending Oberlin College in Ohio for two years, Silas returned to Vermont to study Medicine at home. He finished his education at Vermont's Castleton Medical School, graduating in 1844. That same year, he married Rachel.

After marriage, Rachel suspended her teaching career to manage her household and serve as her husband's business partner. She became interested in medicine then, but no colleges were open to women. She read her husband's medical textbooks and, in the process, taught herself the equivalence of a college education. Rachel also studied and practiced alongside Silas at the sanitarium he had opened in 1846 in a small village on the western border of Allegany County in New York. Silas and Rachel had become intrigued by a medical movement known as hydropathy, which uses water to treat disease or maintain health. It was first developed in Austria in the 1820s. By 1840, several water cure sanitariums existed in Germany and England.

While Rachel continued to study at home, Silas started two other sanitariums in New York state. Rachel practiced for three years at Glen Haven and one year at Ithaca. During this time, Silas became a professor of hygiene at the Central Medical College, an eclectic college in Rochester, New York. Eclectic medicine used noninvasive therapies and healing practices instead of conventional bloodletting, mercury, or other disinfectants to cure severe infections in the 1800s. Eclectics relied on herbs and plants for treatment and closely followed Native American medicine traditions. They believed in the curative power of nature and choosing or selecting the most effective methods and remedies with the slightest toxicity for treating patients. Most importantly, they determined that the lack of sanitation was killing people, which gave rise to the popularity of sanitariums.

When the New York State Eclectic Society held a meeting to plan the opening of a college in Syracuse, Silas attended and proposed a resolution that the college should open its doors to women. Once the resolution passed, Rachel immediately applied and was accepted for enrollment. Prior to graduating from Central Medical College, Rachel gave birth to her first child in 1850 while still a student. Later on, her daughter, Adele Amelia Gleason, also devoted her life to studying and practicing medicine. A year after Rachel graduated from medical school, Silas was persuaded to come to Elmira, New York, to treat an influential local businessman. After Silas restored his health, Fox Holden pleaded with him to remain in Elmira. It wasn't that difficult of a decision for the Gleasons, who found the countryside pleasant and a perfect place to open a sanitarium.

Throughout her role as head of the Elmira Water Cure, Rachel maintained a large and successful consulting practice that extended across New York state. She went from town to town and house to house with her "parlor talks" to educate women about their health. As one of America's first women doctors, she was also one of the first to insist that women naturally understood the health needs of women better than male physicians, who often dismissed a woman's physical ailments as nonsense or due to emotional breakdown.

Rachel often contributed to health journals regarding dress reform, traveling, and women's health. The female patients at the Water Cure were required to wear loose garments since Rachel strongly believed tight-fitting clothing was responsible for many of the common disorders they suffered. Besides giving lectures on physiology and hygiene, she held Bible and prayer classes every Saturday for twenty-five years. Her book *Talks to my Patients—Hints on Getting Well and Keeping Well* was published in 1870. It is still available as a Scholar Select book for "being culturally important and a part of the knowledge base of civilization as we know it."

In other writings, Rachel described her treatment for patients, which she referred to as invalids, as a combination of a simple diet, pure air, regular exercise, and the medical use of water as a tonic for the whole nervous system. Daily bathing was required, and caffeine, alcohol, or tobacco was strictly forbidden.

Rachel was a generous woman who recognized that needed change could best be achieved through education. Before the Civil War, Rachel was an anti-slavery advocate, and afterward, she offered regular assistance to Freedman's Schools tasked with educating freed Blacks. Rachel also paid the tuition for eighteen women to attend medical school. Most women she sponsored were previous invalids she had treated at the Elmira Water Cure.

Rachel and Silas are still remembered as community leaders and pioneers, compassionate healers, educators of health care, and advocates of human rights. The following is from the Memoriam written for Rachel by her daughter:

"In this home, in 1820, was born Rachel Brooks. Here she grew to womanhood and surroundings of unsurpassed natural beauty. Here, with rapidly expanding intelligence, she learned the ways of physical health and useful industry, of plain living and high thinking and beautiful feeling, the fear of God, love of country and home and neighbors, all the great round of human affection, of which father and mother and sister and brother are but the endeared exemplification."

"I often asked her what was the best of life. 'Not honor or success, but knowledge and peace!' And so it was to the last hour: Peace." — Adele A. Gleason

Rachel and Silas Gleason, October 16, 1892, listening to Annis Eastman, wife of Reverend Samuel E. Eastman of Park Church in Elmira, NY. Mrs. Eastman was among the first women ministers in America to be ordained (1898). (Gleason/Bush/Wells Collection)

Elmira Water Cure

The Elmira Water Cure opened its doors on June 1, 1852. The idea of the sanitarium came about in 1850 when Silas, who had already acquired a reputation for treating patients with hydropathy, which uses water to cure diseases, was called to Elmira to assist a patient with a severe case of lung congestion. The man he healed was the previously mentioned Fox Holden, a prominent businessman with considerable influence in the community. Mr. Holden convinced Silas and Rachel to move to Elmira. Silas had successfully run three sanitariums in New York, but none of their locations were as appealing as the Elmira countryside.

With the help of Mr. Holden, it wasn't long before Silas and Rachel found the perfect spot for their new treatment center. It could be easily reached by railroads that ran through Elmira in every direction. There were abundant clear water springs nearby, and patients would have a glorious view of the Chemung River and its valleys from the hilltop where the sanitarium would be built. Chemung is a Native American word meaning "place of the bighorn." The name was given to the river by Delaware natives after discovering the fossil tusk remains of a wooly mammoth along its banks. The carefully selected site overlooked the city, the river, the valleys, and the rolling hills throughout the property, providing miles of beautiful scenery for anyone seeking physical or mental restoration.

Mr. Holden and his friend, Marshall Hale from Phoenix, New York, had a large, chalky structure built for the Gleason's sanitarium on the East Hill, about a mile down the road from Quarry Farm. When Reverend Thomas K. Beecher, the minister of The Park Church, first came to Elmira in 1854, he described the building as "cheap, clean, and honest." He took up residence at the resort for three years. Eventually, he built a cottage across the road from it. Jervis Langdon, who paid half the cost for building The Park Church, purchased Quarry Farm for his family's summer home in 1869. His daughter Olivia married Samuel Clemens (Mark Twain) a year later, and they, too, began spending the summers there.

The main building of the Elmira Water Cure had four stories with two attached wings three stories high. Initially, bath water had to be carried in pails and heated on wood stoves. Later, water from the springs was delivered through wooden pipes to the building. Wood-burning stoves heated the private rooms, but patients had to pay the cost of the wood. Patients also had to provide a blanket, two cotton sheets, one linen sheet, two towels, and table napkins for their use at the resort. The average cost for each patient was ten to twelve dollars a week, which only the well-off could afford back then.

Silas and Rachel practiced what was known as "eclectic" medicine, which is defined as selecting the best solution of all possible solutions when treating a patient. Using water as a cure for diseases was often met with skepticism by traditional medical doctors who had not yet discovered how valuable a proper diet and simple hygiene could help restore a patient's health. Regular bathing and drinking water are the main contributions that hydropathy made to the science of medicine.

An advertisement featured in *Brigham's Elmira Directory* (1963-1964) stated: "We seek, first of all, to CURE OUR PATIENTS. Water is our Chief Remedy. But we do not hesitate to use Homeopathic remedies, Electricity, or any other means within our knowledge to facilitate the recovery of the Sick. We are Eclectic in our practice—using all means that, in our judgment, shall do any good to any patient. Those who come to us shall have the benefit of our best skill and care."

In its early days, the Water Cure was often referred to as a "Tavern for the Sick" or the "Home for Invalids." Later it became The Gleason Sanitarium. Over time, the Gleasons became widely known as healers in their treatment of the sick, the half-sick, and the most difficult of all to treat, in their opinion, those who thought they were sick.

Elmira Water Cure - Advertisement circa 1860

While the Gleasons may have used the same instruments found in the medical bags of traditional doctors, some of their equipment may have seemed unusual or out of place in the general practice of medicine. One such appliance was the electrostatic machine used to cure various ailments, especially rheumatism. This treatment involved a high voltage static charge applied to a patient sitting on a chair or stool atop a platform resting on four-inch-tall legs made of glass bottles sawed off at the neck. The legs insulated the platform's feet to prevent grounding when using the device. Supposedly, jolts of electricity could also improve circulation, minimize pain, and relieve patients of mental anguish.

During the nineteenth century, medical vibrators were often used by conventional doctors to resolve the complaints of women patients. While pelvic massages were intended to relieve female hysteria brought on by sexual frustration, physicians also believed that vibrators could ease other disorders such as constipation, arthritis, and muscle fatigue. By the turn of the century, advertisements for portable electric vibrators could be found in ladies' magazines and catalogs such as *Needlecraft, Woman's Home Companion,* and *Sears-Roebuck.*

Later, vibration therapy using high-frequency and sinusoidal apparatuses was employed to cure muscle spasms, support cardiovascular health, treat indigestion, and calm nerves in anxious patients. There was even a vibrating chair designed to mimic the movement of train and carriage rides, which, its inventor observed, seemed to reduce the discomfort of patients with Parkinson's disease. Oscillator machines consisted of a belt worn around the backside or stomach that would vibrate the patient's body tissue to help reduce weight and other conditions like constipation and atrophy.

Other machines used at The Elmira Water Cure included an ozonizing apparatus for disinfecting water or helping treat respiratory problems and other infectious diseases. Light therapy included spending time outdoors on sunny days or incandescent electric-light baths to treat bone, joint, and skin tuberculosis. Other ailments could benefit, too, since prolonged exposure to light was thought to kill bacteria that caused disease.

The chief remedy employed at the Elmira Water Cure that remained in place throughout its operation was water applied in various ways to relieve chronic or acute illness. Both warm and cold baths were administered, whether full-body or concentrated on the area of concern. Patients were required to take daily baths to promote good hygiene and drink large amounts of water to help remove toxins. Water, good nutrition, living out of doors as much as possible, and observing healthy habits, such as not smoking or drinking, were essential for keeping the body balanced and cleansing the mind. Rachel was convinced that patients who constantly worried about their health did themselves much harm. In her book *Talks to My Patients*, she wrote:

"To talk and think of one's pains is a sure way to perpetuate them, while unnoticed aches, like neglected guests, are soonest to take their leave."

When the Gleasons moved to Elmira, there were no women doctors in Chemung County or most of the country, for that matter. Many women did not feel comfortable discussing their health issues with male doctors, who often dismissed women's complaints altogether, diagnosing their symptoms and behavior as female hysteria. Marginalizing health issues based on gender caused many women not to get the medical care they needed. As more females entered the medical field, they started hospitals and clinics serving only women. The male-dominated medical establishment fought back by calling women physicians quacks, especially those who practiced hydrotherapy and similar treatments. They refused to see them as equals and ridiculed them by claiming women were too delicate for the profession. Such ramblings did not deter women like Rachel Gleason.

The Gleasons maintained that most conditions women experienced were not due to hysteria but to their lack of understanding of how their bodies functioned. Rachel's book *Talks to My Patients* sought to remedy this misconception in its attempt to address all stages of a woman's life. Never before had there been such a resourceful reference aimed at educating women about their health and how to keep it. Long after Rachel was gone, her words still reached out to women, encouraging them to take charge of their well-being and maintain usefulness throughout their lives. A former patient gave this testimony about the care she received from Rachel during her stay at the Water Cure:

"You were my physician, counselor, and friend. Whatever I am, whatever I have accomplished, I owe to the example of your useful, consistent life, Blessed among women."

Over the years, many young physicians interned at the Water Cure. Several of them were women who went on to establish a practice themselves. The Gleasons took a short leave of the sanitarium around 1868 after Silas was prescribed a stay in Florida due to health issues. During their absence, the Water Cure remained open under the care of trusted physicians who leased the facility from the Gleasons. Several reputable doctors are associated with the sanitarium. Rachel's sister, Zipporah Brooks Wales, and her husband, Theron Wales, served as physicians from 1873 until 1897.

Despite its successful reputation, the Elmira Water Cure and similar institutions were often accused of practicing substandard forms of alternative medicine administered mainly by charlatans. One source inaccurately referred to it as "a storefront water cure run by Reverend Thomas K. Beecher in Elmira, New York, that catered to reforming alcoholics and prostitutes." While Reverend Beecher resided at the Gleason Water Cure for a while, he had nothing to do with its operation. Also, most of the patients treated by the Gleasons sought relief from ailments that traditional medical doctors had failed to cure with procedures, often regarded as medical tyranny, like bloodletting, harmful medicines such as mercury and lead, and narcotics laced with opium and cocaine. Many of the patients who came to the Gleason Water Cure were not the degenerates described above but instead notable: Olivia Langdon, Harriet Beecher Stowe, Susan B. Anthony, Emily Norcross Dickinson, May Riley Smith, and others. Although his wife's family were patients of the Gleasons, it is unknown if Mark Twain was ever treated at the Water Cure, but he often stopped by to chat with his friends, the Gleasons.

The Elmira Water Cure operated from 1852 to 1945. After serving over forty years at the sanitarium, Silas and Rachel retired in 1898. Their son Edward, who had served as the business manager for his parents, took over as owner. Since he was not a medical doctor, he hired Dr. John C. Fisher as the Chief Physician. A year later, Silas passed away. Rachel moved to Buffalo to live with her daughter Adele where she died in 1905. Following her death, Edward changed the name of the sanitarium to The Gleason Health Resort, but even today, it is known by its original name, the Elmira Water Cure. Years later, after Edward retired, his daughter Ada held the reins of the resort until she sold it in 1945. The new owner, Mrs. Ada E. McClellan from Rochester, New York, did extensive remodeling to convert the facility into a nursing home. In 1959, what used to be the Elmira Water Cure was razed after being sold to a couple who wished to build a house on the site. Today, the only thing remaining of its 113 years of caring for the sick is Watercure Hill Road, which now passes through a neighborhood of single-family homes.

Edward and Henrietta Gleason driving away from Elmira Water Cure
(Gleason/Bush/Wells Collection)

Mark Twain and Other
Elmira Water Cure Notables

Throughout its existence, the Elmira Water Cure attracted several notable people, which to some degree, helped build its reputation nationally as a viable alternative for treating patients with chronic and acute diseases. One of the earliest prominent guests at the sanitarium was the Reverend Beecher, who came to Elmira in 1854 to serve as the pastor of the First Congregational Church at the request of Jervis Langdon. Langdon made his wealth from the lumber business and coal trade. He was a passionate abolitionist known as the "conductor" of the Underground Railroad. And later, he became the father-in-law of Mark Twain.

Reverend Beecher was never a patient but resided at the Water Cure for three years until his Victorian cottage with a suitable study/library was built across the road in 1857. His wife, Olivia Day, whom he had married in 1851, passed away a year before he arrived in Elmira. He married Julia Jones in 1857, a cousin to his first wife and the granddaughter of Noah Webster, who compiled the Webster Dictionary.

The eccentric Beecher sometimes rode a tricycle with two large wheels in the back and a smaller one up front. He was a frequent guest at the Langdon house and even had a latch key to let himself inside to rest in the big wicker chair by the bay window he favored. When Mark Twain was courting Olivia Langdon, he got to know Reverend Beecher personally. In the third volume of his autobiography, Twain described Beecher as "one of the best men I have ever known."

The family Reverend Beecher was born into had other notable members, including his brother, Henry Ward Beecher, who was considered one of the most influential Protestant ministers of the nineteenth century. Like his brother, he was an abolitionist, and following the Civil War, he turned his attention to the women's suffrage movement. His reputation plummeted due to accusations that he had had an adulterous affair with Elizabeth Tilton, one of the women in the campaign. Although the six-month trial initiated by Mrs. Tilton's husband ended with a hung jury, the unfavorable public opinion centered around the affair never died. But of all of the twelve siblings of Reverend Beecher, the one who stands out the most is Harriet Beecher Stowe, who wrote *Uncle Tom's Cabin*, which is thought to have been the catalyst that began the Civil War in the United States. Harriet occasionally received treatments at the Elmira Water Cure. She strongly supported hydropathy, having undergone treatment at Brattleboro Hydropathic Institution in Vermont due to exhaustion in 1846. Stowe's sister, Catharine Beecher, a noted educator and supporter of hydropathy, moved in with her brother Thomas in her final years, allowing her to continue her treatments at the Water Cure. Catharine passed away in 1878.

Silas and Rachel were close friends of Reverend Beecher and active members of the First Congregational Church. The church's name was changed to The Park Church in 1871, and its new building was completed in 1875. Reverend Beecher remained at the pulpit until he died in 1900. He was replaced by Samuel E. Eastman and Annis Ford Eastman, who had assisted him for the past six years. In 1898, Mrs. Eastman became one of the first American women to be ordained.

The entire Elmira community loved Reverend Beecher and was devastated by his death. Just a few days before, many Park Church members had stood and sang in his presence at the Sunday evening service. A half-hour later, he developed paralysis and fell ill before dying a week later on March 14, 1900. His funeral occurred on Friday, March 16, with over 1,500 people allowed inside and about the same number standing outdoors. Businesses closed, and the streets were deserted. City schools and municipal offices were also closed. At 2:30 pm, the fire alarm bell rang seventy-six times, one bell for each year that Reverend Beecher had lived.

The Park Church published a book containing numerous memorials to Reverend Beecher. Following his funeral, seven Elmira pastors and reverends spoke at a minister's memorial service the same evening. The book also included thoughts and recollections from other clergymen in the community. There were also articles from the press. The *Elmira Advertiser* stated, "There is no Elmira name of higher distinction or held in more affectionate recollection than that of him whose passing out of this life to another has filled the city with mourning." And the *Daily Gazette Free Press* wrote, "His purse was as open as his heart. A ten-dollar bill in his pocket was an annoyance to him until he could find someone to give it to."

Reverend Beecher would continue to live in the hearts of those who had known him for many years. On February 10, 1924, the hundredth year of his birthday, a special service was held at Park Church for both the morning and evening worship. The program cover is believed to be from Aunt Ada, who attended the event with Uncle Bob.

Other notables came to Elmira for treatment as word spread about the Water Cure's success in restoring the health

THE PARK CHURCH
ELMIRA, NEW YORK

SERVICES IN CELEBRATION OF THE CENTENNIAL
OF THE BIRTH OF

THOMAS K. BEECHER

1824 - 1900

WORKMAN · CITIZEN · PHILOSOPHER · MINISTER
NATURE · STAMPED · HIM · BY · COURAGE
CANDOR · LOVE · TO · BE · A · SHEPHERD · OF
SOULS

Thomas K. Beecher, 100th Birthday Celebration.
(Gleason/Bush/Wells Collection)

of their patients. And perhaps, some were attracted by Rachel's involvement in social issues such as abolition and women's suffrage as much as they were by her recognition of women's medical needs at a time when male doctors scoffed at their complaints. While Clara Barton has been tagged as a patient at the Elmira Water Cure, there is no documentation to confirm this. In 1876 she resided at another water cure, the Jackson Health Resort, known as the "Home on the Hillside" in Dansville, New York, after suffering from physical exhaustion. Once her health was restored, Clara organized the first local chapter of The American Red Cross in Dansville, remaining there for ten years. Before becoming a nurse, she was a teacher who started the first free public school in Bordentown, New Jersey. The school was so successful that the town board hired a male principal at twice Clara's salary to oversee it. The enraged Clara resigned after stating her position: "I may sometimes be willing to teach for nothing, but if paid at all, I shall never do a man's work for less than a man's pay." Clara went to work for the U.S. Patent Office as one of the earliest women hired by the Federal Government, and later on, she began her nursing career. Whether or not she stayed at the Elmira Water Cure, she was a strong proponent of homeopathic medicine.

Susan B. Anthony was best known as a women's rights activist who co-founded the National Women's Suffrage Association with Elizabeth Cady Stanton. Her preference for homeopathic doctors was mainly because of their medical protocol and reputation for accepting women into the medical profession. Like many feminists in the nineteenth century, Susan viewed health reform as an essential aspect of the Women's Rights Movement. She was most likely drawn to the Elmira Water Cure because its staff had traditional medical backgrounds despite being open to all forms of medicine, including homeopathy. But she would have also embraced Rachel as a progressive thinker and a champion of women's rights, especially regarding health care.

Other well-known people from the nineteenth century have been mentioned in several newspapers and books as receiving treatment at the Elmira Water Cure, including Emily Norcross Dickinson, the mother of the poet Emily Dickinson, and the poet May Riley Smith. Even a couple of politicians were patients: Schuyler Colfax, the U.S. Vice President under President Ulysses S. Grant, and Congressman Samuel Cox, who was also a scholar and writer. By 1900, over twenty thousand people across America had passed through the Water Cure's doors for treatment. It's difficult to say whether hydropathy's popularity, the medical staff's success in restoring patients' health, or the celebrated patrons the sanitarium attracted lured them in.

Samuel Clemens, better known as Mark Twain, was the most famous person ever associated with the Elmira Water Cure. He became acquainted with the Gleasons following his marriage to the daughter of Jervis and Olivia Lewis Langdon of Elmira. After they married, the Clemens moved to Buffalo, New York, where Samuel was editor and part-owner of *The Buffalo Express*. Still, they spent their vacations at the Langdon family home, Quarry Farm, just a mile up the road from the Water Cure. The Langdons were friends and neighbors of the Gleasons, and both families attended The Park Church. From the time Olivia was a young girl, Rachel was her physician. All four of the Clemens' children were born in Elmira and delivered by Rachel, most likely in the Langdon house. Samuel was so impressed with Rachel that he called her "the almost divine Mrs. Gleason."

It was not unusual for Mrs. Clemens to return to Elmira to give birth; after all, she grew up there and trusted the care she had always received from Rachel. My mother-in-law, Barbara Wells, did the same. She was born and raised in Elmira and preferred to have the doctor who had cared for her following a terrible accident to deliver her sons, who were born almost three years apart.

It is rumored that a few months after Samuel's first child, Langdon Clemens, was born, he summoned Rachel to Buffalo to see after Olivia, who frequently suffered from poor health, and help with her baby son. When Rachel thought she had done all she could, she attempted to return to Elmira, but Samuel refused to hear of it and supposedly barred the door and forbade her to leave.

When Langdon was sixteen months old, his sister Susy, named after her aunt, Susan Crane, was born. Three months later, Langdon passed away after coming down with diphtheria. Olivia could not travel due to her fragile health, and Samuel did not want to leave her alone. They did not attend their precious son's funeral in Elmira. His body was laid out in the parlor of the Langdon home in the same room where the Clemens spoke their wedding vows. In the mid-eighteen-hundreds, the mortality rate for children under five was around 300 out of 1,000 (30%). Samuel Clemens never talked about his son, but he blamed himself for taking Langdon out for a ride on a cold day which may have led to his illness. It is not known how Olivia dealt with her loss. But chances are she would have turned to the woman who understood more than most the impact of emotional stress on one's health, the "almost the divine Mrs. Gleason."

Rachel & Silas Gleason, 1895.
(Gleason/Bush/Wells Collection)

Maple Point Cottage
1895 - 1922

When Edward purchased Maple Point in 1895 at a public auction, he intended to sell it for profit. He had only paid $1300.00 for it even though the previous owner had mortgaged it for $1900.00. Edward had never seen the place until he and his wife Henrietta and their fourteen-year-old daughter Ada decided to visit the cottage on Keuka Lake one afternoon. There was no road on the west side of the lake where Maple Point was situated, so they could either take East Lake Road and row a boat over to the cottage or go to Hammondsport and hop on a steamboat that would drop them off at Maple Point's landing.

Once the Gleasons saw the property, they decided to keep it. The cottage was almost fifty years old and needed improvements but had potential. It was an easy trip from Elmira and would be an idyllic spot to spend the summers. Best of all, Ada could invite her friends to join her at the lake. When they left for home that day, plans were already being made for a fun summer.

Edward and Henrietta had lost their firstborn daughter, Edith Adele Gleason, seven years earlier. Edith was ten years old when she passed away in 1888, and Ada was seven. She was buried in Woodlawn Cemetery in Elmira, New York. Her name, date of birth, and date of death were filed in Chemung County Records. But no obituary could be found, nor any mention of Edith in the numerous accounts written about her well-known grandparents, Silas and Rachel. Edith's gravesite does not bear the expected accolades of grieving parents. According to my husband, Aunt Ada never spoke about her lost sister. Several photographs of Edith were included in a scrapbook compiled by my mother-in-law, but that is all. Yet, no one ever said how ten-year-old Edith died—whether an accident or an illness took her young life. Silas and Rachel were still running the Elmira Water Cure in 1888, but nothing suggests that Edith had been under their care. Nor is there any indication that something went awry, and their silence was to avoid their medical reputation from being sullied. An oil painting of Edith hung on Edward and Henrietta's family room wall in California, serving as the sole memorial of their lovely daughter. Many years later, it made its way back to Maple Point. I always wondered why a girl so full of life on canvas was never mentioned, why her death was a secret. While Edith's life remains a mystery, she has not been forgotten. Since 2005, when my in-laws sold the cottage, the painting has hung on the walls of my homes in Georgia, Tennessee, and Texas.

Henrietta and Edward Gleason in their Pasadena, California home in 1929.
The painting above Edward is of Edith Adele Gleason, their deceased daughter.
(Gleason/Bush/Wells Collection)

Two months after Rachel died, her granddaughter Ada married Robert Brooks Bush on May 4, 1905. Robert, or Bob as he was called, was the son of John James Bush and Frances Brooks Bush, who owned the Bush cottage a half-mile North of Maple Point. The Bushes had three sons, with Bob as the oldest and his younger brothers Gabriel Sayre Bush and Henry Charles Bush. Over the years, Ada and Bob had gotten to know one another during their summers on Keuka Lake. Bob and his buddies would hang out at the Maple Point landing, waiting for the steamboats to stop and let passengers on and off. Once the steamer was on its way, the boys would jump into the lake from the pilings of the dock house, making as much noise as they could to attract the attention of the most admired girl on the lake, Ada Gleason.

In 1906, less than a year after Aunt Ada and Uncle Bob were married, they booked passage on Anchor Line's S.S. Caledonia from New York to Glasgow, Scotland, via Moville, Ireland. Steamships in the early 1900s were the primary means of transporting people and goods across the ocean. They were also a status symbol for wealthy Americans who enjoyed leisure travel to Europe. This trip was the first of many that Aunt Ada and Uncle Bob would take to destinations worldwide. Uncle Bob wrote a lengthy letter to family members detailing their cruise. Future journeys were described in journals he kept daily, if not hourly.

Bridesmaids for Ada Gleason Bush, May 4, 1905. Top Row: Florence Wycoff Upson, Ida Langdon, Dorothy Walter. Bottom Row: Louise Henry Thompson, Nellie Sealy Ingram, Mary Henry Reynolds, Jane Burchard (Gleason/Bush/Wells Collection)

Uncle Bob's father, John, was sent to the Island of Palms, Cuba, in 1910 by the company he worked for to harvest timber. A massive hurricane struck the island, and he was presumed dead. John's son Henry went to Cuba to search for his father's remains, but none were ever found. Most likely, he was washed out to sea by the storm.

John was the brother of the American sculptor Henry Kirke Bush-Brown who was married to the artist Margaret Leslie Bush-Brown. Margaret painted a portrait of Henry Charles Bush in 1889 when he was two years old. Like the one of Edith, this painting now hangs in my home. It features Great Uncle Henry holding a cluster of grapes in one hand and his other hand wrapped around a small rose-colored glass bowl with a white raised floral design. The actual bowl in the painting rests on my fireplace mantel. Robert, Gabriel, and Henry were the nephews of Margaret and Henry K. Bush-Brown.

As a young boy, Henry K. lived with and was mentored by his mother's brother, Henry Kirke Brown, widely known as the father of American sculpture. Later, he also took his uncle's sir name, hoping it would help him gain recognition in the art world. When Great Uncle Henry passed away, my husband acquired two bronze bookends with a mother reading to her daughter on one end and a father reading to his son on the other. As it turns out, the bookends were sculpted in 1914 by his great-great uncle and had been sitting on our bookshelves for many years without our knowledge of who created them.

Henry Charles Bush, 1889, Artist, Margaret Leslie Bush-Brown. (Gleason/Bush/Wells Collection)

Sometime after their father died in the hurricane, Uncle Bob and Henry's brother Gabriel married Matilda (Tillie) Stultz. Gabriel was the sales manager for the Eclipse Division of Bendix Corporation in Elmira, which manufactured automotive parts. When his son Robert Sayre Bush, born on May 4, 1913, was five years old, and three weeks before his daughter Barbara Pauline Bush was born, Gabriel died from the Spanish Flu Pandemic on October 22, 1918. Tillie and her two children moved in with her in-laws, Aunt Ada and Uncle Bob. Eventually, Aunt Ada persuaded Tillie to rent a home down the street from the Thompson family, who owned the lake house next to Maple Point. Aunt Ada also suggested Uncle Bob and Gabriel's younger brother Henry board a room in the house to help Tillie financially. Henry had just returned from serving in the Navy during World War I. The arrangement worked out better than expected. On January 12, 1920, Tillie and Henry were married. Even though Henry was their uncle, Robert and Barbara always considered him their father. Gabriel not only wed his brother's widow and raised his brother's children as his own, but he also managed to fill Gabriel's former sales manager position at the Eclipse Division of Bendix Corporation, which he held until he retired.

By 1922, the steamboat era that was begun in 1835 on Keuka Lake came to an end. Since the Civil War, the companies had competed with each other, transporting grapes to railroads and local or tourist passengers to resorts or cottages along the shore between Penn Yan, Branchport, and Hammondsport. By 1915, all but one steamboat had been taken out of service due to the growing number of trucks, automobiles, and buses that took their place.

Henry Kirke Bush-Brown, American Sculptor
(Gleason/Bush/Wells Collection)

Eclipse Bicycle Salesmen Henry
Charles Bush (on the left). According
to an ad in 1897, the cost for an
Eclipse Bicycle was between $50
and $100 (Gleason/Bush/Wells
Collection)

Maple Point Cottage
1923 – 1949

After settling in California, Edward and Henrietta conveyed the deed to Maple Point to their daughter on August 1, 1923. By then, Aunt Ada and Uncle Bob had been married for eighteen years. Although they had no children., they were very fond of their nephew, ten-year-old Robert and their niece, five-year-old Barbara. Since Aunt Ada's only sister had passed away in childhood, there were no nieces or nephews from her side of the family.

A daily record of life at Maple Point, presumably handwritten by Uncle Bob was begun in 1915 and continued in a second volume until 1938. Many people were mentioned throughout the journal, some more frequently than others. Dr. Arthur W. Booth and his wife Jeannette were close friends with Aunt Ada and Uncle Bob. Dr. Booth was a surgeon who lived and practiced in Elmira and helped start the Chemung County Historical Society. The historical center's Memorial Library was named after him. Each October, usually the second weekend of the month, the Booths hosted an H.P.I. House Party at their summer cottage, Lakeside Orchards. It is unknown what H.P.I. stood for since it was never referenced except by initials, but perhaps it was an acronym for "High Profile Individuals," which the members may have laughingly dubbed themselves. Jervis Langdon and his wife, Eleanor Sayles Langdon, were regular guests at Maple Point and the Booth House Party. Eleanor was called Lee by her husband, friends, and family members. Jervis was the nephew of Olivia and Samuel Clemens. After his aunt Susan Langdon Crane passed away in 1924, Jervis inherited Quarry Farm, where Mark Twain and his family spent several months each year. Halsey and Julia Sayles were frequent guests and friends of the Bushes, Booths, and Langdons. Halsey, a widely known Elmira attorney, was the brother of Lee Langdon. Another prominent figure and friend of those already mentioned was Jervis's sister Ida Langdon, the niece of Mark Twain and his wife Olivia. Ida, whose parents were Charles Jervis Langdon and Ida Clark Langdon, was a professor at Elmira College, known for having helped several gifted students who could not afford to pay for their educations. Ida was also one of Ada's bridesmaids in 1905. Her friend, Georgianna Palmer, often visited Maple Point with her. Georgianna was a music teacher and one of Elmira's most illustrious musicians. Many others were mentioned in Uncle Bob's journals: Merle & Louise Thompson, who also had a cottage close to Maple Point, Bebe Breese, whose parents owned Dogwood Cottage not far away; and a couple only referred to as the Coopers.

Before Edward and Henrietta moved to California, they, along with Aunt Ada and Uncle Bob, would travel from Elmira to Keuka Lake, mostly on weekends. Their friends often joined them for a picnic supper either on one of the surrounding hills, along the roadside, on the lakeshore of beautiful Keuka Lake, and occasionally,

H.P.I. House Party at Lakeside Orchards, October 1941. Top Row L to R): Lee (Eleanor) Langdon, Dr. Arthur W. Booth, Ada Gleason Bush. Botton Row (L to R): Halsey Sayles, Jeannette Booth, Julia Sayles, Robert Brooks Bush, Jervis Langdon (Gleason/Bush/Wells Collection)

even by a brook in the woods. Their explorations sometimes included other areas of the Finger Lakes. They also enjoyed outings near Elmira, such as Quarry Farm, the Langdon residence, and Sullivan's Monument, commemorating the American Revolutionary battle in Newtown, the original name of Elmira. A favorite pastime was attending concerts in Ithaca at Cornell University's Bailey Hall. Whatever they chose to do was always a delight, and everyone was welcome to accompany them.

Good times at Maple Point involved swimming in Keuka Lake's pristine water if it wasn't too cool. Fishing was also a favorite activity, and Uncle Bob kept track of the dates, and the numbers of trout or bass caught each season from 1933 to 1938. Many days were filled with long walks described in the journals, noting the yellow Lady Slippers, the purple orchids they especially admired, or the wild strawberries they gathered. The bluebirds and the beautiful mourning cloak butterflies captured their attention also, and even the black and red fuzzy caterpillars did not go unnoticed. Uncle Bob meticulously recorded what automobile they drove or rode in and who accompanied them. He noted the sudden storms that muddied the mostly dirt roads and sometimes caused them to get stuck or decide to turn around and head for home. For this reason, Uncle Bob often drew maps on the pages of the journal of alternate routes for getting from one place to another. Interestingly, he never described the picnic fare, which seemed to be the highlight of most of their outings, concentrating instead on the scenic location where it was consumed. On one junket, he noted that he, Aunt Ada, and the Booths had stopped by the side of a road with a beautiful view and sunset to have supper "on top of the world."

In addition to his daily journals, Uncle Bob recorded every detail of the trips he and Aunt Ada took, domestic and foreign, in separate diaries. Ida and Georgianna often accompanied them on some of their North American vacations, including Bay St. Lawerence, Nova Scotia, and Mexico. Aunt Ada and Uncle Bob traveled throughout Europe, Australia, New Zealand, Russia, South America, and Africa. Most of their trips occurred after Uncle Bob retired from his sales position at Harris, McHenry & Baker Company, a lumber and millwork manufacturer.

When Maple Point was opened for the summer season in 1935, a new system for registering cottage guests was in place. Uncle Bob would no longer write daily notations about who, what, and when. Instead, guests would sign their names in the newly purchased guest book on the scalloped corner dropleaf table next to the double doors opening onto the front porch. Volume One, which detailed June 1935 to July 1941, was dedicated to "Many Happy Days." Guests could also write short comments about their visit. The usual crowd that appeared in Uncle Bob's journals since 1915 continued to come to Keuka Lake and surrounding areas until their deaths: the Bushes, Booths, Langdons, Sayles, Coopers, Thompsons, Breeses, and others.

The Maple Point guest book was also convenient for noting significant events,

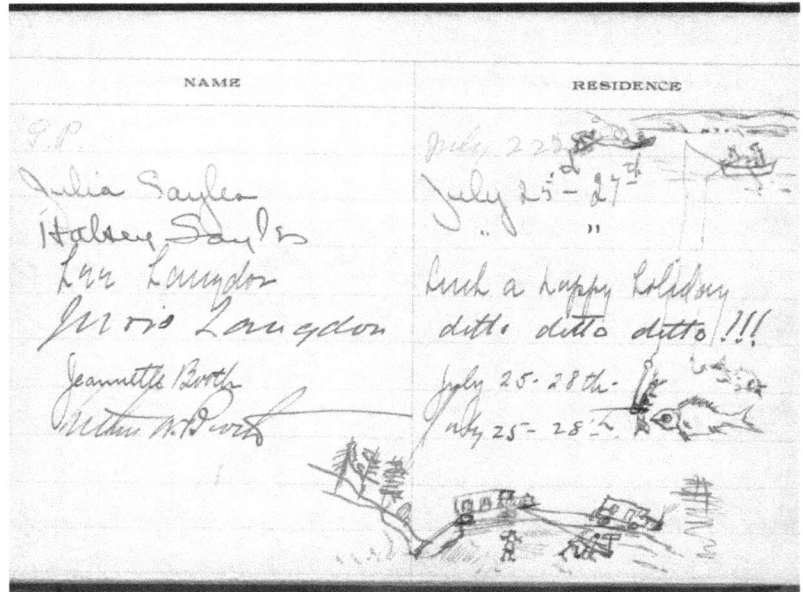

Maple Point guest book, July 1941. It is believed that Robert Brooks Bush did the drawings on the page since similar ones can be found in his daily journals. (Gleason/Bush/Wells Collection)

such as "the big flood of 1935." The rain that began on Friday, July 5, 1935, was the kind that lent itself to a day of reading or playing a round of Bridge. There was no such thing as forecasting the weather among the primary sources of information: newspapers, radios, and telephones. Uncle Bob's brother and sister-in-law, Henry and Tillie, their son Robert and daughter Barbara had come to Maple Point for a long Fourth of July weekend expecting to enjoy the usual lake activities like swimming, badminton, fishing, and canoeing. But the rains continued, and the storms intensified.

On Saturday night, there was a heavy thunderstorm, and while it did not produce much damage, it washed away the paths and part of the road by the gully on the property's north end, which then filled with gravel, mud, and other debris like that scattered about the premises. The grocer from Bluff Point could drive a short distance on the upper road and then walk or row in with food and supplies. He also agreed to collect outgoing mail and drop it off at the post office. His offer prompted Aunt Ada to write letters detailing the storm to her parents.

Some of the neighbors were not as fortunate and had to sweep water and mud that had made its way through the windows and doors. It began to rain and lightning just after dark on Sunday evening, though not enough to cause concern, so Uncle Bob and Aunt Ada decided to get some sleep. In the early morning hours, the rain pounding on the tin roof of the boathouse was so loud that nothing else could be heard. Uncle Bob woke up and went outside, hoping to divert the water overflowing the creek away from the cottage. Aunt Ada, who had not been able to sleep, looked out the window after hearing rushing water as it tore across the yard and flower beds and brought gravel into the boathouse. She quickly put on her bathing suit, cap, rubber coat, and an old pair of shoes and went outside to bring the beach chairs and dock house furniture higher up on the lawn before they floated away. The canoe was half full of water, which kept it from drifting into the lake. When everything had been done, they came back inside for breakfast. Soon after, it poured again for about two hours, causing the lake to rise even more and leaving the point covered six inches deep.

Tillie revealed that she and Henry had stayed up all Sunday night, thinking they would have to escape at any moment. Henry couldn't believe that his brother Bob was sleeping through such a terrible storm instead of worrying about what to do. In the meantime, Tillie agonized over what to wear. While she didn't like getting her best corset wet, she certainly didn't want to be found wearing her old one should the floodwaters carry them off somewhere.

Over the next few days, news of how much damage the flood had caused shocked even those who had experienced it. Aunt Ada commented in one of her letters to her parents that she had never realized how often she went to the dock house and how much she had always enjoyed walking down to it each evening with Uncle Bob to look at the stars and listen to the gentle lapping of the waves against the dock pilings. All of that could have been lost. Forty-four people died during the storms, most of them from drowning while trying to flee campsites or houses swept from their foundations. One woman was electrocuted after trying to rescue a table lamp in her flooded living room. Nearly one hundred and fifty homes and businesses were destroyed. Bridges were washed away, roads and streets were so gouged they were impassable, and train tracks were severely damaged. It had been thirty-three years since a storm of this magnitude had threatened the area.

Maple Point dock house during flood of 1935. Water rose six inches above the point. (Gleason/Bush/Wells Collection)

The following year, Aunt Ada and Uncle Bob's niece Barbara moved into a dormitory at Elmira College, even though it was in the same town where she had lived all her life. The school was founded in 1855 as a private women's college. Later, it was distinguished as the first college for women to offer rigorous academic programs equal to what was taught in the best men's colleges. It did not become coeducational until 1969. In 1983, Jervis Langdon, Jr., the great-nephew of Mark Twain and the son of Jervis and Lee Langdon, appointed Elmira Collage as the guardian of the Langdon family's Quarry Farm, where Mark Twain spent his summers and wrote some of his best-known works.

Alumnae Hall – Elmira Collage, 1917 – 1977 (Postcard)

On the evening of October 2, 1936, shortly after her freshman year had begun at Elmira College, Barbara, and several friends ventured onto the roof of their dormitory, Alumnae Hall, through a door opening from a corridor on the fourth floor. The top center section, which made up the fourth floor, did not extend the entire length of the building on either side, so the girls had a bird's eye view while walking about the third-floor roof.

Several girls who had not joined the others on the rooftop thought it would be fun to lock the door on the fourth floor to prevent them from coming back inside. The girls trapped on top looked for a way to escape and found an unlocked window which they believed opened onto the fourth floor with only a three or four-foot drop. Barbara insisted on climbing into the window feet first, facing backward. One of the other girls held Barbara's wrists as she clutched the sill and lowered herself through the window.

With her legs dangling in the air, Barbara, overcome with terror, struggled to retain her grip. The girl holding onto her tried desperately to pull Barbara back through the window but did not have the strength. As Barbara's hands slipped from her friend's reach, she fell forty feet down a dark empty shaft constructed for an elevator that had never been installed. The girls on the roof were horrified and screamed to attract attention. Help arrived within fifteen minutes, and Barbara was rushed to the hospital. She had multiple severe injuries, including a fractured skull, fractures on both sides of her upper and lower jaws, a broken pelvis, and her right leg was also broken. The close friend of Aunt Ada and Uncle Bob, Dr. Arthur Booth, was Barbara's attending physician. According to Dr. Booth, Barbara's outcome was uncertain, and if she did survive, she had a long road ahead of her.

Barbara remained in the hospital for one hundred days. Even after recovery, Aunt Ada insisted that she not return to Elmira College. It is not known if the college accepted any responsibility for the accident. Alumnae Hall had a low wall around the roof's edge, and the door leading to the third-floor deck was usually locked from the inside, with a key kept in the lock so students on the fourth floor could exit the fire escape in case of emergency. Students often went on top of the roof to relax since there were no restrictions against it.

At the beginning of the next school year, Barbara enrolled in Hood College in Frederick, Maryland. The original name of this private institution was Women's College of Frederick, established in 1893. Its name was changed to Hood College in 1912 in recognition of the generosity of Margaret Scholl Hood, who had gifted the school a twenty-eight-acre tract of farmland in 1897. Barbara majored in Home Economics, and four years later, upon graduating from Hood, she accepted a teaching position at Annapolis High School.

Barbara's older brother, Robert, graduated from Cornell University in 1934 and then did graduate work in meteorology at the Massachusetts Institute of Technology. Robert's first assignment with American Airlines was at their weather station and landing field in Mt. Pocono, Pennslyvania. In 1937, he joined Pan American Airways as a weather forecaster, informing clipper captains of large, long-range flying boats of weather conditions throughout the hemisphere. A year later, he was appointed manager of Pan America's Canal Zone meteorology bureau in Cristobal. On January 22, 1939, he married Alma Louisa Joseph, who joined him in Cristobol a week before their wedding. Not long after that, Robert was transferred to Coconut Grove, Florida. Moving back to Florida meant they could visit Maple Point each year in late spring, as long as he was back at work before hurricane season began.

Although Robert did not serve in the armed forces during World War II, even Meteorologists that were not drafted played a significant role in the war effort. Knowing wind and weather patterns was essential for planning strategic operations, especially those involving spying or surveillance. And even rain and fog were beneficial in concealing tactical movement. Because of this, weather forecasts were restricted or banned to prevent the enemy from gaining information that could favor their military campaigns. One of the best examples of how weather made a difference in the war's outcome is that of D-Day. A brief window of clear weather predicted in the English Channel enabled Allied forces to attack and defeat the German army on Normandy beach in the south of France.

Meteorologists also kept track of potential typhoons and monsoons in the South Pacific that could reap as much destruction as the enemy. Toward the end of World War II, the clippers Robert used to help guide through storms and other weather conditions were being phased out due to an increase in new airports worldwide. As a result, longer routes could be reached at higher speeds in less time and without requiring a water landing.

A new generation began when Robert and his wife Jo (Alma) became parents to twins Henry Brooks Bush and Barbara Gleason Bush in May of 1943. They moved to a rental house in South Miami while waiting to build a larger home two blocks away, which remained their home throughout their lifetimes.

Robert Sayre Bush, 1959, as Division Meteorologist studying a jet stream map at Pan American Airways. (Gleason/Bush/Wells Collection)

Hospitality had always been extended to dogs at Maple Point since Merle and Louise Thompson's chocolate Labrador Retriever Patty began making daily rounds to the cottage. Patty always got Aunt Ada's attention and affection, especially after she showed up with both ears bandaged following a fight with a woodchuck. It would be a while before other pets would visit the cottage, so Patty didn't have to worry about any other dog taking her place.

In many ways, 1943 was an exceptional year, beginning with Barbara's marriage proposal in early January. She had met Lee in 1942 at the boarding house in Annapolis, Maryland, where they both dined. Barbara was a high school teacher, and Lee was an electrical engineering instructor at the Annapolis Naval Academy. One evening in early September, Barbara and Lee had been stood up by their dates, so Lee decided to make the most of it by asking Barbara if she would like to go to the cinema. They also went to the movies the following two nights. It was the last time either of them was stood up, which after all, they considered a testament that some things were meant to be. They announced their engagement on Valentine's Day and were married in Elmira on July 10, 1943. Although it was a small wedding, appropriate for one in the middle of a world war, Barbara wore a traditional long white wedding dress and a heart-shaped cap with a mid-length veil. Following the ceremony, taken from the 1928 Edition of the Episcopal Book of Common Prayer, Lee and Barbara took a train to San Francisco for their honeymoon.

Barbara's Aunt Ada and Uncle Bob invited the newly weds to Maple Point the following year. Lee and Barbara both had a week's leave from their jobs in Annapolis, so they accepted the invitation. Spending time at the lake with Barbara's aunt and uncle was an eye-opener for Lee, and he quickly realized what an advantage it was to have a relaxing place like Maple Point to visit. Aunt Ada and Uncle Bob treated Barbara and her older brother Robert as though they were their offspring. They were generous in all respects, including paying for Barbara's wedding dress and hosting the wedding reception at the Mark Twain Hotel in Elmira.

After serving as an instructor at the Naval Academy's Post Graduate School for several years, Lee received orders to report to Pearl Harbor in the Hawaiian Islands toward the end of summer in 1945. When Barbara was pregnant with her first child, she moved back in with her parents in Elmira while Lee was away. People in Elmira who knew about Barbara's fall down the empty elevator shaft a few years back at Elmira College were surprised to hear that she was expecting. It irritated Lee and Barbara's mother, Tillie, when one of them would ask how Barbara could deliver a baby, considering her previous injuries. Lee didn't think it was their business and could be somewhat frank in reminding them of this.

Soon after Lee arrived in Hawaii, World War II ended on September 2, 1945. Had the war continued, he would have gone to sea for the first time in his naval career as the executive officer of a destroyer. All around, the Bush and Wells families were spared from combat duty. Lee's younger brother, Frank Wells, was deferred from the draft because of his job as a chemical engineer at Eastman Kodak. Likewise, Barbara's brother Robert remained stateside as a meteorologist throughout the conflict.

During the war, guests flourished at Maple Point, and there was never any mention of what was happening overseas. They came to Keuka Lake to escape, and since no immediate family members were engaged in combat, it was easier for them to carry on as though nothing but having a good time mattered.

Although he could have remained in the Navy, Lee was only interested in returning home, finding a job, and waiting for his firstborn to arrive. He stayed in Hawaii until he had enough points to be separated from duty as a full lieutenant at the end of November. His separation took place in New York City. While waiting in a long line at the discharge center, Lee conversed with a young U.S. Navy Aviator Ensign whose father worked for Crocker-Wheeler Electric Manufacturing Company. Lee got his father's name and address and wrote him a letter of application. After receiving offers from all four companies where he had sought employment, Lee accepted a position with Crocker-Wheeler. The only drawback was that he would have to spend six weeks training in New Jersey.

Lee began his training course on January 21, 1946. He temporarily rented a third-floor room in a boarding house and took the train every Friday evening to Elmira and returned to New Jersey each Sunday afternoon. One improvement for Barbara was that her Aunt Ada and Uncle Bob offered their apartment to her once they left Elmira to spend the winter in Pasadena. One morning in early February, Barbara's father, Henry, contacted Lee to tell him that the baby was on the way. Barbara had gone to the hospital the night before, and although it was the afternoon before Lee arrived in Elmira, the baby had still not come. It wasn't until the following morning, February 8, that Lee Arrington Wells III was born.

After Barbara was released from the hospital, she and the baby stayed in Elmira for six weeks before joining Lee in New Jersey. Of course, this meant that Lee had to find a suitable place for all three of them, even though it was for a short time. Once Lee completed his training, he was transferred to Crocker-Wheeler's sales department in Los Angeles. Before heading west, Lee and Barbara and their infant son Lee III spent a week at Maple Point, where a family reunion took place with Barbara's parents, Henry and Tillie, and her brother, Robert, who came up from Miami.

In 1947, Lee and Barbara spent their summer vacation in Roseburg, Oregon, visiting Lee's parents, Florence and Lee A. Wells Sr. Barbara had never missed a summer at Maple Point since she began going there at age four. Knowing that her brother Robert, his wife Jo, and their twins Henry and Barbara, along with her parents Henry and Tillie, were there in early September made her homesick. Although it was never discussed, Barbara had a miscarriage sometime between late 1946 and the end of 1947. Her pregnancy and the miscarriage may have been why she and Lee did not make long-distance travel plans that summer.

1948 brought many changes to the Wells family. That summer, Lee's father fell ill and passed away in late August. Lee was transferred from Los Angeles to Milwaukee at about the same time. Shortly after the funeral, the family packed everything and headed East. Barbara was pregnant for the third time, although Lee did not count the second expected baby since it was never born. He thought it would be good for Barbara to stay with her parents in Elmira until the new baby arrived. That way, she could have the same doctor who delivered Lee III and was familiar with her past injuries. No doubt, Lee was also concerned about the possibility of another miscarriage. Barbara and Lee III left for Elmira soon after they got to Milwaukee. Lee stayed at a hotel until he was able to find an apartment. On October 21, Barbara and Lee III spent a day at Maple Point before her aunt and uncle closed the cottage for the winter. By then, Barbara was two months away from giving birth. Her second son, Robert Bush Wells, was born on December 21st. Lee took a train from Milwaukee to Elmira as soon as he heard the news. Six weeks later, he returned to Elmira to fetch his family and take them back to Wisconsin.

Not long after the family had settled into their apartment, Lee's mother sold her home in Oregon and moved in with him and Barbara. Although she would remain with them for the rest of her life, later on, it was agreed that she would spend the summer months with her other son, Frank Lilburn Wells, and his wife, Joanne, in Rochester, New York. There was another family reunion at Maple Point in 1949. Robert, his wife Jo, and their six-year-old twins arrived on July 9th. The next day, Lee and Barbara, Lee III, and baby Bob, who was now six months old, showed up. It was a grand time for all, with memories constantly being made. The children

Kids Sitting on Log at Maple Point, 1949. (L to R) Jean Wellinghoff, Ginny Wellinghoff, Barbara Gleason Bush, Lee A. Wells III, Henry Brooks Bush Background: Barbara Bush Wells holding Robert Bush Wells. (Gleason/Bush/Wells Collection)

attracted other children from nearby cottages. Maple Point was no longer just a haven for the elite group of friends of Aunt Ada and Uncle Bob but an enchanted playground for the young family members and their friends who were fortunate enough to be there.

Maple Point Cottage
1950 – 1962

When Aunt Ada and Uncle Bob opened the cottage in mid-June 1950, they noted the swallows nesting under the porch, and nearby in the trees, they spotted brown thrushes and red-eyed vireos. North of the porch were robins and phoebes. Bird watching and identifying plants were their favorite pastimes, aside from fishing for bass near the dock house or swimming in Keuka's pristine water if it wasn't too cold.

Tillie and Henry, Robert and his family from Miami, and Lee and Barbara and their two sons, Lee III and Bob, were the first guests to arrive that season. July 15th marked another family reunion which the family hoped to continue yearly. Lee III, who was four and a half by then, was working on learning to swim. He got his head underwater for the first time but hadn't quite mastered the "dead man's float."

Toward the end of their vacation, Lee's brother Frank and his family visited Maple Point for the first time. They also brought Grandmother Wells, who spent the summers with them in Rochester. At the time, Frank and Joanne had two children, Marjorie Lee and Peter. Aunt Ada and Uncle Bob welcomed Lee's brother and his family to visit the cottage the same as they would receive blood relatives. They never felt it was an imposition to have extra people there to enjoy all that Maple Point had to offer, whether for a day or overnight.

It was late August when the cottage was fully opened in 1951. Aunt Ada and Uncle Bob had gone to Europe and were expected back home a few days later. Lee, Barbara, Lee III, and Bob arrived one day before Lee's brother Frank, Joanne, Marjorie Lee, Peter, and the family's new baby, Frank Jr., showed up.

Opening up the cottage could take as long as two days. Fortunately, Aunt Ada and Uncle Bob had a list of everything that needed to be done, with each step performed methodically and for a good reason. The first thing was to remove the heavy wooden bolted shutters that protected the windows from ice storms or break-ins. The pump for the well had to be turned on and primed. During the winter, the water system was shut off, the pipes were drained, and the toilets were sponged to prevent them from freezing. A water sample was then taken to the hospital for testing since chlorine was not yet used for purification.

Next, the porch was swept, and the outdoor furniture had to be moved from the inside to the verandah. The table and chairs stored under the house were brought up to the side terrace, and the beach and dock house chairs were also put in place. Leaves were raked off the walking paths, and shell gravel was used to fill any hollows. Each side of the beach was also combed. The flag pole and pole for the windmill were erected about midway between the lake's point and the porch.

The mailbox, which was removed each winter to prevent any mail from being delivered, was set up, and the septic system was checked to make sure it was working. The boat dock had to be moved out into the water, and the boat's outboard motor had to be obtained from the marina, where it was stored for the off-season. The battery for the car kept in the garage during the cold months was also held at the marina and had to be reinstalled.

The final thing was to go to the grocery store in Penn Yan and stock up on food and supplies. Opening or closing the cottage was hard work, but everyone could relax and enjoy being there once everything was done.

Sadly, Aunt Ada and Uncle Bob's long-time friend, Dr. Booth, passed away on October 22nd that year. His last visit to Maple Point had been in 1950. One month before his death, his wife, Jeannette, came to the lake without him while he attended a meeting in Penn Yan. It is unknown if Dr. Booth's H.P.I. House Party was still meeting each October at Lakeside Orchards or if the members continued the tradition after he was gone.

The last guest of the season in 1951 was a snowstorm that began in early November, which undoubtedly added to the burden of closing Maple Point as Aunt Ada and Uncle Bob prepared for their return trip to California. Most likely, it did not go unnoticed that a new era had begun, one of welcoming the next generation and saying goodbye to those who once held their place.

By 1952, the children of the Bush and Wells families were old enough to participate in most of the activities available at Maple Point. Nine-year-old Cousin Henry claimed to have caught fourteen fish that summer, and his twin sister Barbara went diving in Keuka Lake. Bob Wells, age three and a half made his first attempt at swimming. Lee III must have had a good time because he didn't want to leave. The adults equally expressed how much they enjoyed being at Maple Point and looked forward to their next visit with their gracious hosts who never tired of having constant guests.

By the end of the year, another frequent guest at Maple Point and member of the annual H.P.I. House Party, Jervis Langdon, passed away. According to the Maple Point guest book, the last time he was at the cottage was in 1947. In 1936, Jervis presented Ada & Bob with a signed copy of his "Samuel Langhorne Clemens" booklet, which contained reminiscences and excerpts from his uncle's letters and unpublished manuscripts. Jervis ended his collection of little-known stories of one of America's greatest authors with a comment that echoes the task that I, too, adopted for gleaning the Maple Point guest book for other bits and pieces of what life must have been like over the years: "My attempt in writing down these odds and ends was to depict a little of what transpired in the closer contact of family life."

After Aunt Ada sold the Elmira Water Cure in 1945, she and Uncle Bob traveled extensively worldwide. In early 1953, they took a twenty-five-day journey to Australia and New Zealand that was "believed to be the first organized party of American tourists to come to New Zealand since World War II." Henry and Tillie opened the cottage that year since Aunt Ada and Uncle Bob were off again on a "Coronation Cruise" with stops in several European countries. June 2, 1953, marked Queen Elizabeth II's coronation, and they were eager to see the celebration parade. According to Uncle Bob's journal, he and Aunt Ada left their hotel at 4:15 am to catch a bus to London. Their tour guide had arranged for them to watch the parade from the window seats of a second-floor building along the route. They were served coffee, biscuits, chicken or ham salad, and tea cookies while waiting for the parade to pass. It was 3:15 pm before the procession came around. Many in the crowd had gathered the night before, and it had rained most of the day. Aunt Ada and Uncle Bob waited until most people were gone before returning to the bus stop. Once they reached their hotel, they had a nice dinner celebrating Coronation Day. They did not return from their trip until July 20th. Meanwhile, the "Miami Bushes" arrived at the cottage for their annual visit. Cousin Henry bragged about catching a black bass eleven inches long, and his sister Barbara enjoyed swimming twice a day. After they left, the Wells family showed up. Bob, who was then four and a half, was cast in the year's first play that the Wellinghoff girls who lived down the road presented in their playhouse. The playhouse had belonged to Bebe Wellinghoff when she and Barbara were little girls who played together. Bob was one of the three little pigs who had to confront the big bad wolf who threatened to blow their houses down. Lee III learned to swim that summer, and so did the family's new puppy, Wendy, who liked to chase dragonflies while dog paddling. Wendy was a black and white mixed breed with mostly border collie markings. There was always a dog at Maple Point each summer from that time forward.

Will YOU supply EYES for the NAVY?

NAVY SHIPS NEED BINOCULARS AND SPY-GLASSES.
Glasses will be returned at Termination of War, if possible.
One Dollar will be paid for Each One Accepted.
Tag each Article with your Name and Address and express or Mail to
Hon. Franklin D. Roosevelt, Ass't. Secy. of Navy.
% Naval Observatory - Washington D.C.

WILL YOU HELP US "STAND WATCH" ON A DESTROYER?

The cottage was opened in late May of 1954. Tillie and Henry were the first guests, followed by Robert, Jo, and the twins. Cousin Barbara enjoyed swimming as usual, and her brother Henry caught a twelve-inch pickerel that year. Henry and Tillie enjoyed bird watching as much as Aunt Ada and Uncle Bob, so when they spotted the red-orange tail of a lively America Redstart hopping from one tree branch to another, they grabbed the brass telescope perched on top of the wooden medicine cabinet that hung above the desk in the living room. The telescope had belonged to Aunt Ada's father, Edward, who had donated it to the U.S. Navy during World War I. Due to a shortage of visual equipment, the Assistant Secretary of the Navy, Franklin D. Roosevelt, called on citizens to donate spyglasses and binoculars needed on naval vessels transporting troops or standing watch over American ports. Anyone who participated in the "Eyes for the Navy" program received one dollar for each item they loaned and were promised the return of the equipment whenever possible. Perhaps one of the Navy's posters appealed to Edward and other patriotic citizens to part with their telescopes, knowing they could go down with a ship or get lost in the administrative chaos of war.

In July, the Lee and his family spent their vacation at the lake, and Frank and Joanne and their three children came for a day. That year, the only thing missing was the "Miami Bunch" since Robert, a meteorologist, could not always make the trip during hurricane season.

For many, going to the same place for vacation every year would not be desirable. But no one ever complained about being bored while lying in the hammock or reading a good book on the front porch. The liveliest conversations always took place at the breakfast table, and mornings were reserved for going into town or taking care of routine tasks. The afternoons were spent doing whatever anyone chose to do, whether fishing, swimming, skiing, or playing croquet. Some summers were crowded with guests, and others where hardly anyone showed up.

Nothing significant occurred in 1955, but everyone who visited the cottage that year had good things to say. Mark Twain's niece Ida wrote this in the guest book on September 23th: "One of the happiest, loveliest, and most interesting twenty-four hours I ever had." The same day, the distinguished musician Georgiana visited Maple Point. Perhaps her comments in the guest book referred to Aunt Ada and Uncle Bob's recent trip to Hyannis on Cape Cod: "here, but also abroad with Rob's views." Undoubtedly, the conversation between Ida, Georgiana, Aunt Ada, and Uncle Bob must have been stimulating.

When the Bush and Wells families gathered at the cottage in July 1956, the season's highlight was a fishing trip that Lee III, Bob, and their uncle Robert and Cousin Henry from Miami took early one morning before breakfast. They went out on the lake in a wooden boat with a five-horsepower motor to a quiet cove where the fishing was good. The rods and reels Uncle Robert and Henry brought to the cottage were fancy compared to the bamboo poles that Lee III and Bob had grabbed from the boathouse. Since he was the oldest, Lee III claimed the long rod, leaving the short one for Bob. Bob was six and a half, so no one expected him to be much of a fisherman.

Bob and Lee III dug up their worms, then put them in a wooden box with a hinged screen cover that their great Uncle Bob had made. They filled the box with leaves to prevent the worms from being fried by the sun's heat. The bamboo poles had a fishing line and hook. Bob carefully took a worm, hooked it, and then dropped it in the water. Uncle Robert and Cousin Henry began casting their fancy rods into the water, and though Lee III had a

Bob Wells fishing off pier with Wendy. Sometimes Lee III and Bob would bring the wooden captain chairs from the dining room down to the beach to sit in while they fished. Maple Point, 1956.

bamboo pole, he felt sure he could out fish the others. Soon, Bob got his first nibble and caught the day's first catch. Altogether, he caught five keepers. Uncle Robert, Cousin Henry, and Lee III didn't even get a bite and returned home empty-handed. Once back at Maple Point, the fish heads were cut off with a fish knife and buried in a hole behind the boathouse. After the fish were scaled, they were taken to the pantry. Later that evening, they made a fine meal for all to enjoy.

Later that day, Bob got his pole and box of worms out again. He stood at the end of the boat dock where the water was like looking in a mirror. After getting his first bite, Bob pulled in a foot-long bass. The fish was so big he had trouble landing it and had to call Cousin Henry to help him bring it in. Bob's sixth catch of the day earned him the right to brag about how the youngest fisher with the worse fishing pole outdid everyone else. When telling the story years later, he always pointed out that what mattered the most in life was not what you had but how you used it.

The Bush family from Miami was excited about spending three weeks at the lake in 1957. Robert released the bass he caught out of season but made up for it by snagging two pickerels, nine perches, and one rock bass, enough for three dinners. Cousin Henry hooked a fifteen-inch pickerel and a fourteen-inch bass. Bob pulled in a thirteen-inch bass with his bamboo pole, and Cousin Barbara, who had turned fourteen, caught the attention of a boy across the lake.

Other guests included Henry and Tillie, who stayed at the cottage for five weeks that summer, and Frank, Joanne, and Grandmother Wells, who only spent one day at Maple Point. No matter how long or short a visit, everyone went home refreshed. Earlier in March, Wendy, the dog belonging to Lee III and Bob, died during surgery after swallowing something she had eaten. A few months later, the family got another dog from the Milwaukee pound, and Grandmother Wells suggested that the boys name her Cindy since her coat was as black as cinders. It was noted in the guest book that Cindy "took to the lake as if she owned it."

The day after opening the cottage in 1958, Uncle Bob fell on a slippery spot caused by DDT used to spray the ceilings to control spiders that had dripped onto the floor. After being checked out at the clinic in Penn Yan, it was determined he had only suffered bruises and soreness rather than a broken arm as first suspected. Uncle Bob and Aunt Ada returned to their apartment in Elmira for a couple of weeks. By the time the Wells family arrived in late June, Uncle Bob was much better and even rented a 16HP motor for towing anyone who wanted to ski.

According to their father, Lee III and Bob were not allowed to ski until they passed the swimming requirements he had put in place, including swimming four laps from the dock house to the boat house. Keuka Lake was about one mile wide, meaning that, at the most, they would be a half-mile from the shore if they fell into the water while skiing. Swimming the laps was the best and safest way to build up to that length. Lee III was probably the only one ready to be towed behind a motorboat.

H.P.I. House Party member Halsey Sayles, the brother of Lee Langdon, passed away in 1958. The following year, his wife, Julia, also passed away.

The Wells family opened the cottage in 1959 since Aunt Ada and Uncle Bob were away touring parts of Europe and Russia. They were joined by the Bush family from Miami, who were able to stay three weeks at Maple Point that year. As usual, Frank, Joanne, and their three children visited for one day. Marjorie Lee and Peter enjoyed skiing while their younger brother Frank Jr. had a good time swimming in Keuka Lake. The cottage was temporarily closed since everyone had to leave before Aunt Ada and Uncle Bob returned. Lee had been transferred to his company's Chicago office in the second half of 1958, so the family now lived in Palatine, Illinois. Aunt Ada and Uncle Bob returned from their trip on July 25th and stayed at Maple Point until September 21st. The days were chilly by then, especially since the cottage wasn't winterized.

The former Elmira Water Cure was razed in November of 1959. This well-known landmark where Silas's ashes were scattered would soon be the new owner's private residence. Bob noted that neither his parents nor his great aunt nor uncle ever took him to the Water Cure before it was torn down or shared much of its history with him.

1960 marked the beginning of a new era of protest, revolution, and widespread social change. Despite the upheaval in the rest of the world, the cottage remained steadfast as a haven for all who came to visit that year. Lee, Barbara, and their boys spent their vacation at Keuka Lake and enjoyed seeing Frank and Joanne's family when they visited from Rochester. By then, Frank Jr. was old enough to try out water skiing. That year, the only thing of note was that the Breese cottage, where the Wellinghoffs spent each summer, was struck by lightning on September 21st. Their electric attachments were damaged, and the woodwork was blown out in several places. Fortunately, the strike did not cause a fire, and no one was injured. One tree near the beach was also struck.

In early 1961, Aunt Ada and Uncle Bob traveled to New Zealand, where they had vacationed in 1953. Lee and Barbara opened the cottage in early May. Lee had accepted a position with his company in Syracuse, New York, a couple of months back, and the family was now living in Fayetteville. Being this close to the cottage was a tremendous help to Aunt Ada and Uncle Bob, who turned eighty years old that summer. Lee, Barbara, and their boys could be at Maple Point every weekend. Lee had a three-week vacation, so they could spend it at the lake without driving very far like they did when they lived in Milwaukee and Palatine.

Soon after Aunt Ada and Uncle Bob arrived at Maple Point, they purchased a new boat from Johnson's Boat and Motor Sales. Cousin Henry drove his grandparents from Florida to the cottage in July. The interstate road system was not finished in some areas, and road maps often lacked some of the rural roads needed for the trip. According to eighteen-year-old Henry, there was a lot of anxiety and discussion throughout the three-day drive to Maple Point. Cousin Henry and his grandparents arrived several days before the Wells family. Cousin Henry was anxious to try the fiberglass outboard motorboat but could not persuade Johnson's Boat and Motor to hand it over to him. He had to wait until July 15th, when it was christened "Maple Point," before enjoying it with everyone else, especially those who liked waterskiing. Bob, who had often watched his brother Lee III perform, finally got the hang of the sport, and by summer's end, he had mastered the technique of slalom, which uses only one ski.

Bob and his great-uncle enclosed the lean-to on the side of the boat house with one-by-six tongue and groove lumber framed by two-by-fours and used gravel for the floor. The lean-to was perfect for storing the rowboat and canoe in the winter months.

There were a lot of visitors that year. Grandmother Wells and Frank and his family all showed up. Bruce Wells, a first cousin of Lee and Frank, brought his wife Addie and their children, Patty, Bruce, and John, for a family reunion. It was a wonderful time for Aunt Ada and Uncle Bob, who often felt lonely when everyone left to return home. While Aunt Ada and Uncle Bob had seen much of the world, they also enjoyed traveling throughout the United States. They took a two-week tour of the Grand Canyon and other parks in the western states in August. By August 20th, they decided to call off the remaining parts of the trip due to the altitude, so they stayed at a hotel until they could catch a train back to Elmira. It was October 1 when they began closing up the cottage for the season. After dinner that evening, they returned to Maple Point for the night. Uncle Bob had a fall and had to go to the Penn Yan clinic to ensure he hadn't broken any bones. But overall, 1961 had been an incredible year filled with travel, friends, and family.

By 1962, Lee and Barbara had taken over the task of opening and closing the cottage each season. Aunt Ada and Uncle Bob were coming a little later and leaving sooner than they had in the past. And now that the Wells family lived in Fayetteville, Barbara, Lee III, and Bob could spend the entire summer at the lake. Lee would join them each weekend and when he took his annual three-week vacation. This arrangement also allowed Lee III, who was sixteen, to work at Johnson's Marina once school was out. Another advantage for Lee, Barbara, and the boys was that they could have the cottage to themselves more often, whereas Aunt Ada and Uncle Bob preferred guests most of the time.

One evening in July, while on the lake, Lee III was pulling into a boat dock gas station when another boat ran into him. The young boy who caused the accident was a fourteen-year-old from Camp Arey, a mobile home park across the lake. The kid came around the bend too fast and close to the shore. Fortunately, no one was seriously hurt, just a few sprains but no broken bones. However, the boat purchased one year before was damaged enough that it had to be replaced.

In September, another boat incident occurred about one hundred feet out off the north side of the point in front of the cottage. It was still daylight, about seven-thirty pm, when a rowboat with four men aboard began to swamp due to being overloaded. Two men in the boat couldn't swim, and only two life-preserver seat cushions were on board the sinking vessel. All of the men were intoxicated and nearly drowned. A guest visiting the cottage next door to Maple Point jumped into the lake and helped rescue one of the men. The others managed to get back on shore with the help of another man who had seen what had happened. Lee III and a friend of his, Jim, towed the almost capsized boat onto the beach. Two men returned the following day and moved it away as quickly as possible while Uncle Bob made an example out of the incident as to why "liquor and boats don't mix."

In late September, Aunt Ada and Uncle Bob boarded the SS President Monroe that took them from Jersey City to Los Angeles via the Panama Canal. The passenger/cargo ship, owned and operated by American Passenger

Lines, was previously used by the U.S. Navy to transport troops and supplies to the South Pacific. Soon after it departed on its maiden voyage, it was ordered to return to San Francisco Bay due to Pearl Harbor being attacked. The ship was awarded five battle stars for its World War II services. It was returned to civilian service in 1947.

On board with Uncle Bob and Aunt Ada were three giraffes from Uganda being shipped to the San Diego Zoo. The giraffes had begun their journey on June 1st, traveling from Africa to Germany, Belgium, and then to New York. Topper, a male, and two females named Freckles and Checkers would join two reticulated giraffes from Somali, Waffles and Dolly. The zoo's innovative open exhibit was on a mesa surrounded by a moat that prevented the giraffes from trying to walk or jump over its fence. The first giraffes to come to the San Diego Zoo, Lofty and Patches, were caught in a horrific hurricane on the eastern U.S. coast in 1938. Their crates were severely damaged, and their food was lost in the ocean. As the ship made its way to the shore over the next three days, the cook made pancakes for the giraffes.

The SS President Monroe passed through the Gatun Locks on October 5 and entered the Pacific Ocean the following evening. It was not allowed entry by immigration authorities when they reached, Mexico, on October 11th, supposedly due to the possibility that the giraffes had Acapulco foot and mouth disease, which was prominent in East Africa. The SS President Monroe had to anchor from the shore, and passengers could not debark. It is unknown whether the delay was due to the traveling giraffes or the increasing concern that ballistic nuclear missiles were being constructed in Cuba, just ninety miles from the coast of Florida. Most likely, the passengers aboard the SS President Monroe did not know that the advent of a nuclear war between the United States and the Soviet Union was hanging in the balance as they waited offshore.

Topper, Freckles, and Checkers making their way from Uganda to their new home at the San Diego Zoo aboard the SS President Monroe in October 1962.

After much red tape, the transporter ship was allowed to continue its journey to California, where the giraffes and passengers were happy to be on land again. Toppers, Freckles, and Checkers were quarantined for several months before joining Waffles and Dolly sometime in 1963.

Maple Point Cottage
1963 – 1971

On June 6, Aunt Ada and Uncle Bob took a train to Chicago on their way to Elmira for the summer. Other than going to the cottage, they had no travel plans. Their health was failing, and it wasn't easy to get around. Aunt Ada had to have a wheelchair once they got off the train. A friendly Red Cap ensured they were comfortable, took them to the station restaurant, and helped them onto the Erie train to Elmira.

Lee and Barbara met the train in Elmira and drove Aunt Ada and Uncle Bob to Keuka Lake to get their car out of storage, where they kept it each year during the winter months while they were in California. Next, they went to the apartment that Barbara's aunt and uncle maintained year-round in Elmira, although they were seldom there. According to Lee, Uncle Bob seemed curiously excited and told them that Aunt Ada had something important she wanted to discuss with them. Lee and Barbara were quite surprised when Aunt Ada offered them the cottage. Lee insisted that ownership should be in Barbara's name since she was the blood relative to Uncle Bob. Even though Aunt Ada and Uncle Bob would no longer be responsible for owning the property, they could still visit the cottage yearly. Had Lee not been working in Syracuse, it would have been difficult for Barbara and him to accept the offer.

Around this time, it was becoming evident that Uncle Bob should give up driving, but no one was brave enough to tell him. When Uncle Bob's younger brother Henry, and his wife Tillie visited the cottage in August, Lee and Henry talked it over on the beach one afternoon. They both agreed Uncle Bob should stop driving, but Lee had not counted on being the one the rest of the family thought should take away the keys.

One weekend, before Lee attempted to talk to Uncle Bob, the family decided to have dinner at the LaFayette Inn in Geneva, about twenty-five miles away. Lee III drove his parent's car with Bob in the front and Barbara and Tillie in the back. Lee and Henry rode in the backseat of Uncle Bob's vehicle. The ten miles on the narrow road into Penn Yan went smoothly, but Uncle Bob began to speed when he reached the main road to Geneva. He ignored Aunt Ada when she tactfully tried to slow him down by stating that it was such a lovely afternoon with the sun out, so there was no need to hurry. The road was flat most of the way, and from the backseat, Lee saw a car coming toward them that disappeared from view as it dropped into a gully. Uncle Bob was straddling the center line as the approaching vehicle went over the hill and honked, barely missing them. Aunt Ada raised her voice this time, and Lee and Henry worried about having to ride back home if Uncle Bob was at the wheel. After dinner, everyone stood up, and Uncle Bob graciously handed the car keys to Lee, who never had to say anything about his driving.

Later, Uncle Bob asked Lee III, who had recently acquired his senior driver's license in New York, if he would drive Aunt Ada and him to Elmira one afternoon. Lee advised his son to make sure he accepted the opportunity. For the rest of the summer, Lee III was his great aunt and uncle's chauffeur, which made everyone happy.

As owners of Maple Point, Lee and the boys began to maintain and improve the place. Lee III and Bob ensured the pantry's wood box was always full. Electric heaters were installed to warm the upstairs once Lee had arranged for a service entrance switchboard with more capacity. Lee, who came to the cottage on weekends, kept the dock house in good order and built a railway and carriage for the boat, driven by an electric motor with a "worm" drive that provided automatic breaking once the toggle switch was shut off. Barbara, who did all the cooking and general upkeep, decided it was time to get a washer and dryer. Previously, laundry was dropped off in Penn Yan, where a lady washed, dried, and folded all the things Uncle Bob had inventoried before putting them in a large laundry basket. The new appliances fit nicely in the pantry.

Flares were set out along the lake's edge each Labor Day, creating a Ring of Fire. David Guernsey, who lived across the lake from Maple Point, was dating Jean Wellinghoff, whose grandparents owned Dogwood Cottage. As he went home in his motorboat late one night over the holiday, he saw that the pilings below the dock house on Maple Point had caught on fire. David found a bucket, filled it with lake water, and doused the flames. Everyone at the cottage was sound asleep and knew nothing of the fire David had kept from spreading until he called them to report what had happened the following day. Fire was always a concern at the lake since the lots were heavily wooded. On Independence Day and Labor Day Weekend, many cottagers built bonfires, lit torches, and set off fireworks.

When they closed the cottage for the season in late September, Barbara expressed her thoughts in the 1963 Guest Book: "As new owners of Maple Point, we feel most appreciative, proud, and thankful to be able to carry on. We leave this autumn day with a feeling of nostalgia but know next year there will be many more happy reunions with Aunt Ada, Uncle Bob, and the Miami family."

Aunt Ada and Uncle Bob stayed at their apartment in Elmira until the end of October. Uncle Bob, whose emphysema was getting worse, had to go to a clinic in Hanover for testing throughout the week. Their friend Jane Cooley drove them there and back. On October 28, they left Elmira to board the train to California.

Even though they no longer owned the cottage, Uncle Bob and Aunt Ada were determined to continue spending the summers at Keuka Lake. Sometime around 1960, Aunt Ada began giving her niece Barbara and her nephew Bob who lived in Miami, a check for one-thousand dollars on her birthday, not theirs. She also insisted on paying the property taxes for Maple Point for the remainder of her life.

Uncle Bob and Aunt Ada's journey to Elmira in 1964 went well until a storm knocked down some wires across the train tracks outside Chicago. As they waited, the lights went dead in their sleeping car, so they had to use flashlights to find their bedroom. After a three-hour delay, the train began rolling again. Upon arriving in Elmira, they went to their apartment and later to Ed and Bebe Wellinghoff's home for cocktails before dinner at the Elmira Country Club. The Wellinghoff's daughter Jean was getting married on July 4th.

For the first time, Lee III, nearing graduation from high school, invited his girlfriend, Sue, to Maple Point in April before the cottage was opened. Sue was a freshman, the same as Bob. Later, Sue came for a weekend and coaxed Bob into helping her study for final exams. On his bus ride to school a few days after, Bob recalls seeing "Lee + Sue" painted on the school's water tower in bold letters, though Lee denied having anything to do with it.

Barbara and Aunt Ada attended a bridal shower for Jean Wellinghoff on the porch at Dogwood Cottage on Keuka Lake a few days before her wedding. The marriage ceremony was held at Garrett Chapel, followed by a reception under a tent on the beach at Dogwood. The officiating minister stayed overnight at Maple Point and had breakfast there the morning of the wedding.

The Little Chapel on the Mount, Crypt Door of Garrett Chapel. (Photo taken by Robert Bush Wells)

Known as the Little Chapel on the Mount, Garrett Chapel is located on Bluff Point overlooking Keuka Lake. It was built as a memorial for the son of Evelyn and Paul Garrett, Charles Williams Garrett, who passed away from tuberculosis at age twenty-six in 1929. The Garretts ran one of the country's largest wine-making companies, and the chapel is on the National Register of Historic Places list. The acclaimed artist, Federick Wilson, designed the stained glass on the windows and the crypt. The images on the beautiful bronze crypt door, where the Garrett family is interred, represent the human activities of art, agriculture, music, painting, science, and astronomy. Garrett Chapel is open to the community each summer from July 4th to Labor Day. This peaceful, wooded hillside chapel is a favorite venue for weddings each season.

Uncle Bob took pictures of Jean and David's wedding with his German 35mm Zeiss Ikon camera. When he wasn't able to unload the film, he became frustrated. Nothing like this had ever happened before. Barbara and Bob took the camera to a shop in Penn Yan to see if they could do anything with it. A few days later, the shop owner informed them that the film had been loaded backward, so it was not exposed. It disappointed Uncle Bob greatly, who had captured life's moments on slides for many years. The wedding photos were the last images he would ever take.

Most of Maple Point's visitors in 1964 included Lee's mother, Florence, his brother Frank and his family, and several friends of Barbara. Cousin Barbara , the daughter of

Robert and Jo of Miami, came to the cottage to celebrate her recent college graduation. Barbara got her diploma after three years of study.

Aunt Ada and Uncle Bob returned to Elmira in early September, and Lee III began his first semester at Syracuse University, majoring in art. Lee and Bob closed the cottage on October 4 without Lee III's help. Barbara mentioned what a beautiful day it was as she signed out of the guess book, but perhaps she missed her oldest son, adding it was "always sad to close for the season."

A few days after the closing, Aunt Ada and Uncle Bob's long-time friend, Ida, passed away on October 9. Ida was a professor and the Chairman of the English Department at Elmira College. In 1952, she had her Uncle Mark Twain's study moved from Quarry Farm to the campus of Elmira College. It was in this small, octagonal sanctuary that Twain wrote *The Adventures of Tom Sawyer, The Prince and the Pauper, Adventures of Huckleberry Finn*, and a number of his other works. Moving the study to the campus allowed public access to this historical attraction while maintaining privacy for the occupants of Quarry Farm.

At the end of April 1965, while still in California, Uncle Bob slipped in the bathtub and had to go to the hospital by ambulance. He was in good shape by June 10th when he and Aunt Ada arrived by train at Elmira for the summer. Now that Lee III was away at college, Bob drove his great aunt and uncle to Elmira and back as needed. However, Barbara would accompany them since Bob was only sixteen years old.

Perhaps the summer's most memorable guest was Aunt Ada and Uncle Bob's great-niece, Barbara. Cousin Barbara married Marshall Walter on July 30, 1965, and the newlyweds spent part of their three-week honeymoon at Maple Point. As the story goes, Barbara and Marshall occupied the large, charming upstairs bedroom overlooking the lake, and Aunt Ada and Uncle Bob slept in the bedroom at the other end of the hall. The cottage was not air-conditioned, so keeping the windows and doors open allowed cross-ventilation. Aunt Ada, a practical woman, failed to understand why a newly married couple might prefer having their door closed throughout the night. Uncle Bob, hoping to prevent Aunt Ada from complaining at the breakfast table, suggested that it would be much cooler if the doors remained open. Who prevailed in this matter is unknown, but it was always a favorite Bush family story.

After one year as an art major at Syracuse University, Lee III flunked out, and his vision of being a car designer ended. He had not anticipated that the college curriculum would include more than drawing and designing automobiles, which he had the aptitude and aspiration to do. His downfall was due to the thickness of the art history book he was required to read and comprehend rather than a lack of talent. Unsure of what Lee III should do next prompted Lee and Barbara to consult with the interim president of Keuka College, a private women's school on the lake shore. Dr. Wilbour Saunders advised them to gather all of Lee III's educational records, get in the car, and drive to all the colleges in central New York. He explained that many times the number of first-year students enrolled falls short of what the school had anticipated, and they would be most happy to accept a student standing in front of them with a checkbook in hand. The very next day, Barbara and Lee III did just that. By the end of the day, Lee III was accepted at Ithaca College as an Economics major.

In February of 1966, Robert's wife Alma Louisa passed away from cancer in her home in Miami. She was affectionately known as Aunt Jo by her nephews, Lee III and Bob. In his journal on February 18, Uncle Bob noted, "we were all saddened by the news from Miami." His last entry was in March, believed to be because of his declining health. Aunt Ada and Uncle Bob did not come to the cottage that year. And though the usual crowd of visitors to and from Maple Point came and went in 1966, nothing would ever be the same.

Another loss for Aunt Ada and Uncle Bob that year was that of Jeannette Booth on November 1, 1966. Jeannette was the wife of the late Dr. Booth. She had been active in the Elmira community for many years. After her husband passed away in 1951, Jeannette supported her friends however she could. She often met Aunt Ada and Uncle Bob at the train station when they arrived in Elmira each summer or would drive them to the station when it was time for them to return to California for the winter.

On February 3, 1967, Uncle Bob passed away in Pasadena, where his remains were cremated at the Lamb Funeral Home. His ashes were returned to Aunt Ada, who continued to live in their home with the help of her housekeeper and cook, Faith, her driver, Ollie, and several other attendants.

It was a busy summer at Maple Point, with many guests in and out. Lee III's girlfriend, Kathleen Crowe, stayed at the cottage in August, and Frank, Joanne, Peter, and Frank Jr. came twice that year. Joanne even took some of the creeping myrtle that covered the shaded grounds between the driveway and the gully to transplant in her yard in Fairport, New York.

After graduating high school in late spring, Bob spent the summer working at Johnson's Outboard Motors. His tasks included pumping gas, cleaning boats, sweeping the showroom, and helping build a new warehouse above the road. Bob and Lee III put together new railways and boat lifts for the cottagers on Keuka Lake. In early September, Lee III returned to Ithaca College, and Bob began his first year at Rensselaer Polytechnic Institute in Troy, New York.

With the Vietnam War looming over the head of every eligible male in the country age eighteen and above, Bob decided to apply for the Navy ROTC program to avoid being drafted and sent off to army boot camp. If his draft number was low, he would most likely be selected to serve upon graduation from RPI.

Barbara spent some time in Florida visiting her mother and father in early June. Tillie and Henry had not been to the cottage since 1962. They had always enjoyed coming to Maple Point and often brought their grandchildren, Henry and Barbara, who lived in Miami, with them.

With Lee III and Bob off to college in September, Lee and Barbara felt all alone. Lee kept busy painting the shutters and a few other chores on his list of things to do. Lee III was home for the weekend in October and helped his parents close up the cottage for the winter.

In the summer of 1968, Bob took an eight-week Navy ROTC cruise on the minesweeper USS Dash from Charleston, South Carolina, to Norfolk, Virginia. On his first night at sea, a fire broke out in the engine room, which soon filled with smoke due to a bad bearing on one of the diesel engines. While at Norfolk, he had an opportunity to attend a "rules of the road" and "firefighting" school related to ships.

While Bob was away, Lee and Barbara went to California to visit Aunt Ada. There had been several problems with some of her help, so Lee sorted them out and ensured everything was running smoothly before he and Barbara returned to the cottage.

Although Lee III's girlfriend, Kathleen, lived with her parents in Chicago, Illinois, she frequently visited friends who owned a cottage across the lake from Maple Point. Sometime between 1967 and the summer of 1968, Lee III proposed, and Kathleen accepted. In August, Lee, Barbara, and Lee III flew to Chicago for Lee and Kathleen's engagement party. Kathleen was attending a private school in Pennsylvania, but they planned to marry as soon as Lee graduated from Ithaca College in May 1969. Kathleen came back to Maple Point with them for a two-week visit.

May 17, 1969, marked Lee III's commencement ceremony at Ithaca College. On May 31, a pre-wedding get-together at Maple Point was attended by Grandmother Wells, Frank, Joanne, Peter, and Frank Jr. Lee III left a week early for Chicago, and the rest of the family came up a few days later for the June 14 wedding. Kathleen's family lived in Lake Forest, Illinois, where her father was a corporate attorney. She was the second-born but oldest daughter out of nine children and the first to get married. Lee III and Kathleen's elaborate Catholic wedding took place in the early evening, followed by a sit-down dinner reception at the country club. Although underage, Bob gave the Best Man Toast with style.

Following their honeymoon in St. Thomas, Lee III and Kathleen spent a weekend at the cottage, where they took a romantic moonlight canoe ride across Keuka Lake. Lee already had a job lined up with Carrier Corporation in Syracuse, and to avoid being drafted, he enlisted in the Army Reserves. Two months after his wedding, he set out for summer camp.

A new decade began in 1970 with snow and ice on the lake. It was the end of March before Lee and Barbara could ensure the cottage had no damage. However, they did notice that the no-trespassing sign at the top of the road was gone. Bob was home from RPI for spring break, and Lee III returned from reserve duty.

On March 30, 1970, Barbara's mother, Tillie, passed away. The next day, Barbara and Lee flew to Miami for the funeral. Bob had to return to school, and Lee III, had to return to his job in Syracuse, so neither could attend their grandmother's memorial service. Tillie could best be described as resilient. She was orphaned at twelve years old after her parents died from different causes not that far apart. Tillie and her sister Pauline moved in with their older married sister, Zelia Kretchman, her husband Charles, and their three-year-old son, George. Tillie's brothers, Henry and George Stultz, took over their father's piano business, later known as the Stultz Brothers Piano Company, in New York City. When Tillie was eighteen, she and Pauline left New York City and boarded a train for Elmira. They had both finished secretarial school and were hired by the American LaFrance Fire Engine Company. Not long after that, Tillie met Gabriel, her first husband who died in 1918.

When Lee III and Kathleen came to help open the cottage in late April, they brought their new kitten, Cerina. Lee and Barbara's dog Cindy wasn't thrilled initially, but Cerina and Cindy eventually became friends. Bob came to Maple Point as often as possible for weekend visits until he left for a Navy ROTC summer cruise in the Mediterranean in late July aboard the USS Francis Marion, an amphibious landing flagship. He first flew to

Rota, Spain, and from there, the French Riviera and then to Italy, where the Marines on board practiced beach landings on one of the islands nearby. While on a shore tour near Athens, Greece, Bob rode a donkey down the side of a mountain. When he got back on the ground, a photo of him on the donkey was ready for purchase.

Barbara and Lee, in the meantime, vacationed in Gananoque, Canada, with their friends, the Travers. Gananoque is located in the heart of the Thousand Islands and was considered "a destination of healing and peace" by the Native Americans who once lived along the river banks. When they returned, Lee began building a new bridge over the gully, which he finished before the cottage was closed in October.

1971 was pivotal for the Bush and Wells families, almost equal in sorrow and celebration. In January, Lee and Barbara's fourteen-year-old dog Cindy was put to sleep due to paralysis in her hindquarters. Cindy had been a big part of Lee III and Bob's childhood.

When the cottage was opened in late April, it snowed enough to stick to the ground for a brief time. Lee III, and Kathleen, who was several months pregnant, spent Mother's Day with Lee and Barbara, bringing a pretty plant and cake for the occasion. Plans for buying a new boat were also discussed.

Bob was commissioned in the Navy on June 10 and graduated from RPI on June 11, 1971. Earlier, Bob was awarded the designation of Distinguished Naval Graduate by the Navy Contract ROTC Program. The award was based on outstanding leadership qualities, high moral character, noteworthy achievement under the training program, and exceptional attitude for the naval service.

Another member of the former H.P.I House Party, Eleanor (Lee), the widow of Jervis Langdon and the sister of Halsey Sayles, died on June 15.

In early July, Lee and Barbara decided renting a boat before buying one would be a good idea. Bob drove his parents to Ft. Lauderdale in his car, and Lee III and Kathleen flew down to meet them there. They rented a thirty-six-foot cabin cruiser and spent one week trying it out. Afterward, everyone but Bob flew back to New York. Bob drove to Athens, Georgia, where he would begin training at the Navy Supply Corps School. Once he became a Supply Corps Officer, his duties would include being responsible for providing a thousand meals a day on the ship, paying officers and crew twice a month, foreign exchange, retail operations at the ship's store and snack bar, laundry, spare parts and supplies, and overseeing the officer's stewards.

Once they were back at Keuka Lake, Lee and Barbara bought a thirty-eight-foot wooden Pacemaker similar to the cabin cruiser they had rented in Florida. They kept the boat's original name, "Misty," and stored it at Alexandria Bay in the Thousand Islands.

On August 20, Lee and Barbara bought a new puppy from the Cooks, who lived on East Lake Road. The female dog was one of ten pups whose father was an AKC Golden Labrador and mother an AKC German Shepherd. They named her Bonnie.

Five days later, on August 25th, Kathleen gave birth to Lee A. Wells, IV. Three family members having the same first name was sure to complicate matters. Lee IV was the first child of Lee III and Kathleen, the first grandchild of Lee and Barbara Wells, the first nephew of Bob Wells, the first great nephew of Robert Bush, and would have been the first great, great nephew of the late Robert Brooks Bush.

On August 28nd, Aunt Ada passed away at her home in California. She was ninety years old and would long be remembered for her generosity and good common sense. There had never been any doubt that she was the family's matriarch. Lee and Barbara flew out to Pasadena to handle the necessary arrangements. Like her husband, Aunt Ada was cremated. Lee and Barbara brought Uncle Bob's and Aunt Ada's ashes back to Elmira. A week later, Lee IV was christened in Syracuse. Barbara noted in the guest book that there was "joy and sorrow all in one week."

On September 11, 1971, the family gathered for Aunt Ada's memorial service with burial at the Woodlawn Cemetary in Elmira. It was the first time Henry, Barbara's father and the widowed husband of her mother, had come to Maple Point in eight years. Cousin Barbara had not been up since her honeymoon in 1964. Robert and his wife Jean, whom he married after his first wife Jo had passed away, Cousin Henry and Bob were also at the service. The gravesite for Uncle Bob and Aunt Ada is not far from where Mark Twain is buried.

Fortunately, Aunt Ada and Uncle Bob were cremated before the 1980s. Lamb Funeral Home was a family business for three generations. When the great-grandson of the original owner took over the cremations, things went haywire. First, he undercut the price of cremations to the point that he monopolized the cremation business in Pasadena and surrounding areas. He altered the authorization form so families would not realize they gave him consent to remove tissue when detaching pacemakers from a body before cremation. Soon, he grabbed eyeballs, hearts, and brains from the deceased under the guise of "tissue." The cremation ovens at Lamb Funeral Home were burning bodies night and day. He often stuffed as many as eighteen dead people into one of two ovens. To his way of thinking, the family would never know whose ashes they had or that the box contained a mixture of numerous bodies. Eventually, he was discovered and jailed for his horrendous deeds.

Aunt Ada's passing prompted the daughter of a woman who had known her parents to contact Barbara regarding a sterling silver teapot the woman had given Aunt Ada as a wedding gift. The woman had plucked the teapot from a silver service set that belonged to her family. When the daughter contacted Aunt Ada sometime after the wedding to see if she would return her mother's gift, Aunt Ada made it clear that she felt no obligation to do so. The daughter likely saw Aunt Ada's obituary and assumed Barbara would willingly turn over the teapot. Barbara, however, remained firm about the teapot being a gift and should stay in the Bush/Wells family.

Lee III and Kathleen helped close up the cottage in early October. At six and a half weeks old, baby Lee IV beat the record for being the youngest little visitor to Maple Point. It was an enjoyable time and a reminder that life is cyclical. Although Aunt Ada was the last direct descendant of Silas and Rachel, the birth of Lee IV marked a new generation for the Lee Wells family.

Maple Point Cottage
1972 – 1982

The cottage was opened for the season in late April once the lake was clear of any ice. The water level was very high for the first couple of weeks, up to the corner of the boat house. That didn't bother Bonnie, the pup, who enjoyed continuously going in and out of the lake.

On June 18, Lee and Barbara traveled to Rochester to hear their nephew, Peter Wells, preach a sermon. Peter had recently been ordained as a United Church of Christ minister. A few days later, the great flood of 1972 began, almost as if it, too, was ordained.

Hurricane Agnes, which triggered the flooding, was a category one storm to which most paid little attention. It was expected to veer into the ocean once it hit landfall in Florida, but instead, it turned inland, spawning several tornadoes across the Florida panhandle, Alabama, and Georgia. As the storm approached the Carolinas, it was downgraded to a tropical depression. But Agnes wasn't finished and continued slowly traveling north along the Atlantic Seaboard, bringing heavy rains to Pennsylvania and New York. Six to twelve inches of rain fell over these areas, already soaked from previous rains the week before.

The rains began falling on June 20th in the Southern Tier of New York, overwhelming the streams and rivers and continued until June 25nd. It was the worst flooding ever in the eastern United States. Many lives were lost, including three men surveying the damage when their helicopter clipped a powerline, causing them to crash into Crosby Creek near Hornell, New York. Everywhere trees were uprooted, and some roads were washed out. The storm's center was above Elmira, where city authorities were banking on the Chemung River to stay below flood stage. After three days of torrential rainfall, the river rose to the top of the dikes. Evacuation began that evening, and residents were told to flee their homes before the skies were lit.

The water was higher at Maple Point than during the Flood of 1935. The old croquet lawn and the rest of the point were covered entirely, as was the dock house floor up to the railings. The water rose past the windmill pole, and the boat house was nearly underwater. The Wellinghoffs lost their boat house, but fortunately, the damage and storm debris was minimal at Maple Point.

By early July, the lake had dropped about a foot to where the dock house pilings could be seen. By the middle of the month, motor boats were allowed back on the lake, and the swimming ban was lifted.

Barbara's father, Henry, came from Miami to Maple Point for almost two weeks in August. He and Lee rebuilt the dock house that the flood had damaged. Barbara enjoyed his visit and wished that both Lee III and Bob could have been there to see him. It would be the last time he stayed at the cottage.

While Lee III was away on a two-week Army camp, Kathleen and Lee IV visited her family in Chicago. August 25 marked Lee IV's first birthday. Although Lee III missed this milestone, at least he had seen his son take his first step before leaving for camp.

Bob was on a North Atlantic cruise aboard the USS Pawcatuck AO-108 that began in Scotland and then went to Denmark, the Netherlands, Norway, Germany, and back to Scotland. In early August, the Pawcatuck anchored at Kristiansund, a municipality on the western coast of Norway. On August 6th, the ship headed north across the Arctic Circle at Longitude 5° 12' E, where those aboard received a BlueNose certificate for having passed the gateway to the top of the world. Only one-tenth of one percent of the entire population on Earth has been above the Arctic Circle. The most junior officer and the most junior seaman on the Pawcatuck kept a long-time tradition by painting the nose of the ship blue in honor of the occasion. Norway's Minister of Defence, Alv Jakob Fostervoll, hosted a formal dinner for the officers on board the vessel at a hotel in Kristiansund, where he was born and had served as a councilman and deputy mayor before being elected to the Parliament of Norway.

On their last trip to the cottage before closing it down for the winter, Lee III, Kathleen, and Lee IV joined Lee and Barbara for supper with Bebe and Ed Wellinghoff. The Flood of 1972, which had caused so much devastation for many of their neighbors, was barely mentioned by the end of the season.

The 1973 season was one of those years that could have gone unnoticed. Nothing particular happened; guests came and enjoyed the serenity of the lake and the humbleness of the cottage, while those who spent most of their summers there often sought vacations elsewhere. Early on, Lee III took part in a canoe race in Auburn, New York, while Kathleen and Lee IV visited family in Florida, and Grandmother Wells spent Mother's Day at Keuka Lake.

It had been ten years since Lee and Barbara had taken over ownership of the cottage; time for several improvements to be made. Lee installed a new General Electric double stove that everyone agreed made excellent hotcakes. New toilets, one "Harvest Gold" and the other "New Orleans Blue," were also installed, a new dock was built, and a new roof was put on the garage.

In June, Cousin Barbara, her husband Marshall, and their children, Wade, age four, and Lauren, age one, spent a few days at Maple Point. Lee IV was almost two years old and enjoyed having his first cousins, once removed, there to play with him.

Lee and Barbara celebrated their thirtieth wedding anniversary on July 10th at The Lafayette Inn in Fayetteville, New York, an eastern suburb of Syracuse. Lee, Kathleen, and Bob were there to celebrate with them. Bob was on leave and had not been to the cottage for two years. He was scheduled for a five-month Mediterranean cruise at the end of July.

On August 6, Lee and Barbara flew to San Francisco and drove up the Pacific Coast to Victoria. Once they returned from their trip, they enjoyed swimming in the lake and hosting several guests. Rear Admiral William Kuntz (retired 1972) and his wife Joan spent one night at Maple Point before they headed out for a boat trip on Alexandria Bay, located in the beautiful Thousand Islands.

Lee had known Admiral Kuntz since World War II when they were post-graduate school instructors at the Naval Academy in Annapolis, Maryland, where they taught commissioned officers how to be engineer officers of Navy ships. At that time, Kuntz was a lieutenant commander, but by the time he ended his thirty-year Navy career, he had risen to the rank of rear admiral in charge of the Pentagon's communications. Lee and Barbara played bridge regularly with Admiral Kuntz and Joan and remained good friends with them for life.

When Bob was in his senior year of high school, he applied for a full scholarship in the ROTC program, which would have paid for his college education. He asked Admiral Kuntz for a reference and flew to Washington, D.C., to meet him in person. Bob was greeted at the airport by a young woman who gave him a tour of the city. That evening, Bob had dinner at the Kuntz's home and played bridge with them afterward since he was staying overnight. Although Admiral Kuntz provided the ROTC with an excellent reference letter, Bob was not selected for the program. But fortunately, Aunt Ada made sure the cost of Bob's education at Rensselaer Polytechnic institute was covered.

During 1974, Kathleen, Lee III, and Lee IV continued coming to the lake every weekend when possible. Lee IV became interested in fishing and caught his first bass alone. He also enjoyed swimming in an innertube that summer. He was unaware that he would soon have a brother or sister.

When Lee and Barbara celebrated their thirty-first anniversary, Lee III and Kathleen surprised them by having the canoe refinished. The canoe had been around since Aunt Ada and Uncle Bob owned the cottage.

Frank and Joanne were able to visit on the first of August. Most of the other guests that season were friends of Kathleen and Lee III.

The summer of 1974 marked Bob's honorable discharge from the Navy's active duty. He continued three more years of inactive reserve duty and was promoted to lieutenant by the end of his service. Bob decided to remain in Jacksonville, Florida, where he was stationed, so he toured the state before he began his civilian job at Atlantic Bank as an internal auditor.

Lee & Barbara took a two-week trip in August in their cabin cruiser up the St. Lawrence River. They kept their boat at the Bonnie Castle Resort and Marina at Alexandria Bay, New York, on the St. Lawrence River. Their neighbors in Fayetteville, Jim and Carolyn Travers, accompanied them, which gave them two-line handlers for going through the locks.

After they returned, they visited Widmer Winery in Naples, New York, with Ed and Bebe Wellinghoff. Widmer Winery had been open for over a century. Its founder, John Jacob Widmer, came to Naples, the heart of the Finger Lakes, from Switzerland in 1882 and planted his first vines the following year. He began making wine in his basement in 1885, selling mainly to Swiss folks living in Rochester. Over the years, his wine became so popular that he had to purchase grapes from vineyards outside the Naples area.

Brenton Thomas Wells was born on Christmas Eve, three months after the cottage was closed for the season.

When the cottage was opened in 1975, baby Brenton was four months old when he first visited in early May. Kathleen and Lee III attended Marjorie Lee Wells' wedding in Rochester on May 24 and later celebrated their sixth anniversary on June 15th. The Fourth of July was spent at the cottage with Frank and Joanne, and Bob visited for the first time in two years. Several times throughout the summer, members of Kathleen's family, the Crowes, visited from Chicago.

While projects were always going on each year at Maple Point, none was more welcome than the picnic table for the side terrace that Lee built using plans he had seen in a building magazine. The tabletop was made of two-by-fours held together by lag bolts and was supported by a wide leg on each end with a lateral piece running between the two legs. A turquoise umbrella blocked the sun, and the table could easily seat eight people. Wooden chairs had to be brought down from the kitchen when eating outside, but it was well worth the effort since the picnic table was everyone's choice for dining whenever the weather was good. The only drawback was that the table had to be dismantled and put in the root cellar when the season closed and reassembled the next.

Barbara's father passed away in Miami, Florida, on October 21, 1975. Perhaps the best and most honest description of her Uncle Henry who raised her and her brother Robert as his son and daughter was his keen sense of responsibility.

1976 marked the Bi-Centennial of the United States of America as an independent republic. There were celebrations all across the country leading up to July 4th that year. And on Alexandria Bay, there was also an oil spill. The spill occurred on June 26th when an oil barge ran aground in the American Narrows off Wellesley Island, rupturing three storage tanks. The St. Lawrence Seaway was flooded as 250,000 gallons of crude oil leaked for over a day, making it the most massive inland spill in U.S. history. Wooden boats were porous enough for the oil to penetrate them, so many had to be scrapped. On July 4th, Lee and Barbara drove to Alexandria Bay to check on their cabin cruiser, "Misty." Apparently, despite being made of wood, there was no damage caused by the oil spill. However, perhaps this near-miss led Lee and Barbara to replace "Misty" with a fiberglass boat. Their new boat was a forty-one-foot fiberglass Hatteras which Lee had seen in a Wall Street Journal ad.

Lee III, Kathleen, Lee IV, and Brenton were at the lake most weekends. Grandmother Wells spent the fourth of July at Maple Point, and several of the Crowes, Kathleen's family, also paid a visit. Bob was able to come in August, and in late August, Lee and Barbara went to Rochester for a reunion with Lee's cousins. The weather was cooler than average, with a fair amount of rain. Poor Bonnie got stung on the nose by a wasp, little Brenton had to have hernia surgery, and an old basswood tree had to be taken down; aside from that, everyone enjoyed their summer.

Anyone living in upstate New York in 1977 would long remember the "Blizzard that Buried Buffalo." Syracuse, where Lee and Barbara lived when not at the cottage, was the snowiest city in the country, averaging 103 inches a year compared to 84 inches in Buffalo. No one was prepared for what would become the worst storm on record. The snow began falling on Christmas Day in 1976 and continued to drop a few inches of new snow each day for the next month. The storm began on January 28, 1977, dumping ten feet of snow in one day. The snowdrifts measured thirty feet high, making roads impassable and burying automobiles, rooftops, and anything else on the ground. The temperature fell to zero degrees, but with winds up to seventy miles per hour, it felt like 50 to 60 degrees below. Buffalo was the hardest-hit area, with 199.4 inches of snow accumulated by the time the storm had passed. The storm, no doubt, got Lee and Barbara thinking of moving to a warmer climate once Lee retired a year down the road.

It was Memorial Day weekend before Lee and Barbara, grateful for the warm eighty-degree day, opened the cottage that year. About a week later, one of Aunt Ada's longtime friends, Louise Thompson, passed away at ninety-six. Ada and Louise had spent many years at Keuka Lake, and Louise had served as one of Ada's bridesmaids.

In July, Sally Wellinghoff, the youngest daughter of Bebe and Ed Wellinghoff, was married. Lee III and Kathleen attended the wedding since Barbara did not come to the lake that weekend.

A couple of weeks later, a project was begun to shore up the porch underpinning and build a workshop underneath. The new space would have block walls, a concrete slab, windows, and a garage-type door. Lee even painted the floor and waterproofed the outside walls.

Once Lee was on vacation from work, he and Barbara went to Marco Island, Florida, to check on the house they were building in preparation for Lee's retirement. They would still spend several months each summer at Keuka Lake. This way, they could enjoy boating year-round. Their new home would have a screened-in swimming pool and a canal out back where they could keep their Hatteras.

Lee IV had his sixth birthday party at his home in Cazenovia, New York, rather than at the lake that year. Lee and Barbara came up for the celebration.

In early September, Frank and Joanne brought Grandmother Wells to Maple Point so she could return with Lee and Barbara to Syracuse for the winter.

It rained steadily in early autumn, causing the water to rise more than usual, with nine inches in just twenty-four hours on September 25th. When Lee and Barbara went back to check on the cottage in early October, some high wind and rain had caused a tree to fall across the road near Bebe and Ed's place. Lee III came up to help his parents close the cottage on October 22. Barbara expressed disappointment with the lack of autumn color due to so much rain.

Lee retired from Carrier Corporation on March 1, 1978. He had worked for one company his entire career, beginning with Crocker-Wheeler Corporation, which merged with Elliott Company and was later absorbed by Carrier. The first thing they did following Lee's retirement party was to drive south, stopping in Williamsburg, Virginia to do some sightseeing and then on to Petersburg, Florida, where they would live on their Hatteras until their house in Marco Island was completed. St. Petersburg was about a hundred miles from Marco Island, but it was the only place they could find a covered slip on a marina.

After opening the cottage in early May, Lee and Barbara soon found themselves in a whirlwind of activity, moving some of their belongings from Syracuse to Maple Point. In early June, the movers arrived to pack the remaining contents of their home for their move to Florida. Once the moving van was loaded, Lee and Barbara drove to Marco Island to close on their newly built house. They had sold their home in Syracuse around the same time and would close on that property on July 21st.

In the meantime, Lee III, Kathleen, Lee IV, and Brenton were moving to Birmingham, Alabama in June, where Lee III was starting a new job. When Lee & Barbara left Florida after closing on their house, they stopped in Alabama to see how things were going. They would undoubtedly miss having Lee III and Kathleen around to help them open and close the cottage each year.

Once Lee and Barbara were back north, they caught a plane to Washington, D.C. to help bring their friend Russ Egleston's boat to Syracuse. Despite how busy their summer was, Lee and Barbara were well aware that moving a boat for any distance required help. No one who did any boating would ever refuse to help out unless they had a bona fide reason.

There were only a few guests in August and September. Bob came up from Jacksonville, Florida for several days in August, and Grandmother Wells visited in September. This year, she would fly from Rochester to Marco Island in mid-October to stay with Lee and Barbara from fall until mid-spring.

When Lee and Barbara opened the cottage in 1979, they found two large oak trees downed near the boat house. Most of the summer was devoted to projects. Jerry Thompson, whose family had owned the cottage next door for many years, installed electric baseboard heat and added new electrical outlets throughout the house. The boat house was replaced along with the steel railway sections damaged by the trees. A wooden beam that holds up the front from the root cellar to all across the kitchen was replaced with thirty feet of steel-I beam. The chimney was repaired, and the underside of the dock house roof was overhauled. With all the activity going on, there were no guests at Maple Point that year until Frank, Joanne, and Grandmother Wells paid a visit in September.

When it was time to store their boat for the winter at Kelley's Marina, Lee and Barbara decided to trade it in for an eighteen-foot indoor/outdoor Fiberform MerCruise that was cream-colored with maroon stripes. It had a much quieter engine than their previous boat and a much smoother ride. It wasn't long before they had to take the MerCruiser back to the marina for winter storage, but it gave them something to look forward to when they returned the following season.

After closing up the cottage, Lee and Barbara headed for the auto-train station in Virginia that would take them to Florida. It was much more relaxing not to deal with traffic and driving fatigue when going back and forth between Marco Island and Maple Point.

Just one year after moving to Alabama, Lee III and Kathlene's marriage had fallen apart. Kathlene moved to Granville, Ohio, with her two sons, Lee IV and Brenton. Lee IV was eight years old and knew enough to be impacted by his parent's divorce. Brenton was only four years old, most likely bewildered and unable to understand his new circumstances fully. Sometime in 1980, Lee III started his life over by accepting a position in Tulsa, Oklahoma.

Bob also made a change by moving to Houston, Texas and beginning a new job at First City Bank. Neither Lee III nor Bob realized how their moves would impact them in the future. It is never until we look back that we see how the road we took, instead of any other, made all the difference in our lives.

The first visitors that year were Cousin Henry, his wife, Marjorie, and their six-year-old daughter, Elizabeth Sayre Bush. Henry had not been to Maple Point since Aunt Ada's memorial service in September 1971 and wanted to ensure that Elizabeth got to experience what a special place it was.

Bob spent a week at the cottage, overlapping a couple of days after Lee III showed up with his boys and Anne, his new girlfriend from Tulsa. It had been three years since Lee III had visited Maple Point, and he had a long list of things to do and show his special guest. Lee IV and Brenton enjoyed being back at one of their favorite places. Brenton was now almost the same age as Lee IV had been when their parents separated.

Lee and Barbara's neighbor Norm Thompson repaired the upper garage that they let him use to store his boat. The cottage would get a new roof when they returned the following season. There was also a new sign installed at the top of the driveway. Keeping up the cottage was an ongoing project.

After taking the auto-train, Lee and Barbara arrived at Maple Point on the morning of May 26, 1981. As usual, Bebe Wellinghoff had lunch waiting for them at her cottage. They headed a week later to Frederick, Maryland, for Barbara's 40th Hood College Reunion.

In addition to a new roof, Lee and Barbara also bought a new Buick with a diesel engine, which Lee claims got good mileage.

The only guests in 1981 were Wynn and Bernie Somers, friends of Lee and Barbara in Marco Island.

Before closing the cottage, Lee and Barbara took an Amtrack trip to Houston and Tulsa in September to visit Bob and Lee III in their new homes. Once they returned to Maple Point, they only had a few days before they left on October 1st for Marco Island.

When Lee and Barbara arrived at the cottage on May 26, 1982, they found the long list of improvements and repairs they had written the previous season waiting for them. It was one of those summers when not much was happening, but no one ever complained about not having something to do.

In August, Lee III and the boys spent a week at Maple Point. Lee IV learned how to ski, and Brenton tried his hand at surf sailing with neighbor Jerry Thompson. In late August, Lee's former boss at Carrier Corporation, Vic Pooler, and his wife came over for lunch and spent the afternoon at Maple Point.

Lee and Barbara left on October 2nd for Marco Island. The leaves were falling, and much of the hillside was covered. They had enjoyed a lovely, quiet summer and looked forward to returning the following season.

Maple Point Cottage
1983 – 1989

Soon after the cottage was opened at the end of May 1983, hail the size of marbles covered the entire ground, making it appear like a layer of snow. Overall, the first part of summer was warmer than usual, reaching into the nineties.

Lee III and the boys arrived in July for a week's visit. Aside from fishing, swimming, and skiing, Lee IV and Brenton discovered the fun of playing croquet on a challenging course with many obstacles. The court was initially off to the side until pine trees took over the area, so it was moved to the point.

I met Bob in September of 1982, and three months later, he proposed on New Year's Eve. Our wedding was scheduled for August 6th in Houston, where we both lived. When planning our honeymoon to Montreal and Quebec, Canada, Bob suggested that we also spend a week at Maple Point. I was not keen on this idea since I had never met Bob's parents and felt uncomfortable sharing my honeymoon with his family. As it turned out, Lee and Barbara had booked a cruise from Houston to the West Coast following our wedding since they would be celebrating their 40th anniversary. Even so, I wasn't that interested in going to the cottage. Little did I know it would become my favorite place, "my sanctuary, then and now."

My introduction to Aunt Ada began with my engagement. When Bob asked me to marry him, he took a ring from his pocket that had belonged to his great aunt. It had an old-fashioned platinum setting with two round, European cut diamonds, each three-quarter carets, set side by side at an angle. Although Bob intended to have a new ring crafted using the twin diamonds, he preferred to have me involved in its design. Working with two diamonds proved difficult, so I decided to stick with the angled setting like the original for the engagement ring but with a gold band and a ring guard featuring a semicircle of baguets surrounding each stone serving as the wedding band.

The day after our wedding, Bob and I flew to Syracuse, New York, where we spent the night. The following day, we rented a car, drove to Montreal for a couple of days, and then to Quebec, where we stayed at the Château Frontenac, which proved as elegant as its reputation. Our week in Canada passed quickly, and soon we were on the road again to a place called Penn Yan in New York.

As we drove down East Bluff Drive from Penn Yan, I marveled at all the lake houses in every size and style you could imagine. Ten miles down the road, Bob slowed as we approached a wooden garage and mailbox beyond a driveway with a steep downhill. A tangle of trees hid the cottage from view, and the ground was covered with dark, lush myrtle. We pulled up to the unattractive rear entrance of a two-story house sheathed with cedar shingles, darkened by age. Bob quickly pointed out that the front of the cottage faced the lake and was much more charming than the backside.

We entered the cottage through the back pantry, which it and the kitchen used to be a fishing shack. On the right was a wooden countertop with silverware drawers and cabinets below and built-in cabinets above, filled mainly with gadgets, tools, glass jars, and anything else that required a storage place if ever needed. The refrigerator was across from the washer and dryer Lee and Barbara had added once they owned the cottage. Also, there were recycling bins that Lee managed as meticulously as Uncle Bob had inventoried the laundry that was dropped off in Penn Yan each week on the way to Acme Groceries, followed by stopping at the local fruit stand on the way out of town.

While Bob primed the pump of the well so we would have water, I walked about the cottage, taking note of every room's curiosities. All the walls were dark paneling except the kitchen, which had been painted yellow years ago. My first impression was that the interior was cluttered but humble; it wasn't meant to be stylish. Some of the furnishings were antique, but even the more modern pieces, selected for durability and comfort rather than sophistication, were somewhat worn.

Bob and I had stopped in Penn Yan on our way to the cottage to pick up a few items for dinner and breakfast the following morning. I was glad we had decided on sandwiches rather than trying to cook something. I noticed there were no countertops in the kitchen, and the dishes and pantry items were stored in the tall, floor-to-ceiling cabinets that lined the wall next to the electric stove and oven with a smaller range above the cooktop. The only place to prepare food was on the kitchen table. The sink had a small counter space on either side, but the drain pipe was fully exposed since no cabinets were underneath. The kitchen was rustic but had served the cottage well for many years.

Bob and I slept in the large guest room upstairs with two double beds. The exposed brick of the downstairs chimney occupied the room's southeast corner, which was adjacent to one of the beds. There was no closet, only a shelf above the bed with a long rod underneath for hanging clothes. There were windows overlooking the south terrace on one side and a view of the point along the front wall windows. The windows were kept open since there was no air conditioning, though it rarely got warm enough to warrant it. All through the night, I could hear the gentle lapping of the waves against the dock house. It was very dark since there were no exterior lights, with only the moon shining on the lake. As I drifted to sleep, I heard the bats flapping their wings in the attic as they went in and out through holes under the roof's eaves. For me, it was unnerving; bashing bats with a tennis racket like Bob and his brother used to do if they came inside the house was not how I wanted to spend my honeymoon.

On one of our outings, we went to Niagra Falls, about twenty miles from Buffalo, New York. We also visited Garrett Chapel on the wooded bluff overlooking Keuka Lake. We made trips into Penn Yan but mostly enjoyed the peacefulness of the lake from our view from the porch. The day before we were supposed to fly back to Houston, Hurricane Alicia beat us home. Not wanting to get to Houston and have to stay at the airport if there was significant street flooding, we booked a new flight for a day later. We made it home without problems, but our wooden fence was partially blown down.

Once we were home, a poem about the cottage and the lake gathered in my head. I wrote it down on a parchment sheet using my calligraphy skills, which I decorated with colored ink. Once framed, it would make a good Christmas gift for Lee and Barbara, who had invited us to spend the holidays with them in Marco Island, Florida.

When Barbara and Lee returned to Maple Point following their cruise, they hosted a flurry of guests throughout September. Despite it being a shorter stay than usual due to their travel to Houston and then to California, they had managed to have a new bridge built across the gully on the path to the upper garage and mailbox, and they had also taken the canoe to Kelley's Marina to be refinished. They decided to give the old row boat used to get to and from the cottage before there was a road to Bob Pinckney Jr., whose grandfather founded Pinckney Hardware in Penn Yan.

According to Barbara, 1983 had the best weather she ever remembered, with days mainly in the mid-seventies, perfect for playing croquet.

In March 1984, Barbara's brother, Robert, passed away at seventy years old. He was survived by his second wife, Jean; his son, Henry; his daughter, Barbara; his grandson, Robert Wade Walter; his granddaughters, Elizabeth Sayre Bush and Lauren Gleason Walter; his sister, Barbara; his nephews, Lee III and Bob; and his great-nephews, Lee IV and Brenton. Bob flew to Miami, Florida for his uncle's funeral. I stayed behind in Houston since I did not have enough vacation days to make the trip.

When Lee and Barbara opened the cottage in 1984, they were surprised by the beautiful, late-blooming dogwood trees they rarely saw upon their arrival each year. The lake was high, up to the edge of the dock house, which would delay having the cribbing repaired. But the ash tree in the front yard could come down once they lined up a tree surgeon.

Bob and I had not planned on coming to Maple Point that year since we had visited his parents at Marco Island during the Christmas holidays. Grandmother Wells had been unable to attend our wedding in Houston, so the first time I met her was in Florida. Lee III and his boys also visited Lee and Barbara at Christmas. I had met Lee III since he was Bob's best man, but not Lee IV and Brenton. Lee and Barbara had arranged for Bob and me to stay at a nearby hotel, and Lee and his boys slept on the Hatteras docked in the canal behind the house.

Grandmother Wells had been blind for several years, but she continued to knit to occupy her time and even wove a blanket for our wedding gift from her. Despite a dropped stitch here and there, it was remarkable how skilled she was. Every afternoon, Grandmother Wells would retire to her room. I sensed that she was doing that to stay out of everyone's way, so I made a habit of tapping on her door and asking her if she minded having any company. Grandmother Wells asked me to sit next to her. She traced my wedding ring with her fingers while I described it to her, then gently stroked my face as if she were drawing a picture. We had a delightful time sharing stories of our lives, my favorite being her courtship with her husband, Lee Arrington Wells, Sr., who had died three weeks before Bob was born.

Maple Point

Each morning at Maple Point,
The sky, modest of her glory,
Blushes as the flag is raised in full array.
Sunlight filtered through stained glass
Yields bright colors that dance across the room
To celebrate the day.

The crisp air nudges the woodbine
And a bird's song echoes in sweet resound,
While myrtle leaves, laden with dew,
Hide chipmunks scurrying across the ground.
The cottage, wise and stately
Like the trees that grace her weathered face,
Looks out across the lake,
Now shimmering in the sun's embrace.

The hammock, nestled on the porch,
Offers a panoramic view of canvas water
Painted with sailboats and billowing clouds.
From across the lake: children's laughter and
The sounds made by swimmers and ski boats;
The smell of Sunday barbeques—
Become a shroud from city life and world crises.

The eerie sound of the night owl's rebuttal to the quiet
Is as constant and sure as a recycled moon.
The waves lapping against the boat dock
Lull us to sleep with hypnotic tunes.
And even in our dreams, we know where we are.

Patricia Taylor Wells

On July 8th, Lee's mother, Florence Lilburn Wells, passed away at Rochester General Hospital several days after falling down the stairs at Frank and Joanne's home in Fairport. A memorial service was planned for July 11th at the United Congregational Church of Irondequoit, where Frank and Joanne worshiped, with her grandson, Reverend Peter Wells, presiding. Florence was ninety-six years old when she died.

Following the memorial service, the family gathered back at Frank and Joanne's home. Lee III and his sons had come to the lake several days before Grandmother Wells passed away, and Bob's cousins Peter, Frank Jr., and Marjorie Lee had also come home for the service, so I got to meet them. We only stayed at Maple Point for a few days. It rained one day, so we played Monopoly and worked on one of our favorite jigsaw puzzles, Members of the Court of King Charles VI, with Lee IV and Brenton. I liked my new family very much and looked forward to seeing them the next time we could all be together.

At the end of July, Lee and Barbara flew to Marco Island to bring Grandmother Wells' ashes back after she was cremated. They held a short interment service at St. Mark's Episcopal Church Memorial Garden on Marco Island. On August 10th, they returned to Maple Point for the rest of the summer. By the time they closed the cottage on October 1st, their neighbor, Jerry Thompson, had finished their new garage, and Lee had put in an overhead door for it. Barbara was happy the leaves were turning earlier than usual, providing beautiful scenery for their trip South.

Toward the end of 1984, I resigned from my job at Aramco. Bob and I wanted a family, and now that we could live off his salary, it seemed like a good time.

Lee and Barbara arrived in 1985 with a list of projects for the summer, all of which were accomplished by the end of the season. They replaced the twenty-two-year-old refrigerator with a Whirlpool and added a portable dishwasher. It had always been a chore to wash the dishes in the undivided sink with only a small amount of space for the drying rack. The new dishwasher had a butcher block countertop, making it a convenient place to keep the toaster. Once the dishes were loaded in the washer, it was rolled over to the sink and attached to the faucet by a rubber hose. Lee took charge of how the dishes were stacked inside the new appliance, rearranging them if Barbara or I misplaced anything. Lee finished installing the lights and an automatic door opener for the garage. The front porch got a new roof, and the dock house flooring was completed.

Bob and I came to the lake at the end of June. Bob was interviewing for a job at a savings bank in Hartford, Connecticut, so he arranged his meeting while we were at the lake so I could also explore our potential new residence.

Before we left for Connecticut, the husband of one of my college friends, who lived in Rochester, New York, visited us at Maple Point. William was a French doctor who came to the U.S. after marrying my friend, Kathy. Kathy was in France then, seeing her in-laws, so she could not accompany William. We had a nice lunch and then sat on the porch despite it being cool enough for a sweater. The summers in the Finger Lakes were sometimes more like the winters we had in Texas, chilly but still comfortable.

Lee III and the boys did not come to the lake that year. Bob and I took advantage of not having to divide our time with family members aside from Lee and Barbara. We spent time at Garrett Chapel, which we had also visited on our honeymoon, and then went to Widmer Winery. We toured several historic homes in Penn Yan since Barbara was a docent at one of them. When we weren't sightseeing, we painted the weather vane mounted on a pole overlooking the point and worked on any other tasks needed.

On our way to Connecticut, we stopped in Troy, New York, where Bob graduated from Rensselaer Polytechnic Institute, the oldest private university in the country, founded in 1824. Troy is considered the birthplace of the Industrial Revolution and is nicknamed the "Collar City" because of its history in textile production, especially collar making. It is also known as the hometown of Uncle Sam, the mascot of the USA. As the story goes, Samuel Wilson, a local nineteenth-century meatpacker who lived in Troy, shipped meat packed in barrels to U.S. soldiers preparing to go to war with Canada in 1812. When asked who had supplied the rations, the answer was "Uncle Sam," so named because he employed many of his nephews. The barrels were stamped "U.S." to designate their origin but quickly became synonymous with Uncle Sam, the supplier.

Bob had a short meeting at our hotel in Connecticut with the head of Internal Audit, who had been out sailing that afternoon and showed up late and casually dressed. The following day, they met at the bank for the official interview, after which Bob quickly decided this was not a good fit for him. As we drove through several beautiful neighborhoods, Bob and I concluded that even if it had been the perfect job, we probably couldn't afford to live in Hartford.

Before returning to Maple Point, we decided to tour Mark Twain's Hartford home and gardens. This American High Gothic home was built in 1874 next door to another famous author, Harriet Beecher Stowe, who was known for writing *Uncle Tom's Cabin*. Stowe was the brother of one of Mark Twain's best friends in Elmira, Reverend Thomas K. Beecher. Twain considered Hartford the most beautiful city he had ever seen. Unfortunately, Twain felt compelled to move his family to Europe due to poor financial investments in 1891. Eventually, the house he loved became a museum that some call Hartford's "pride and joy."

Barbara and Lee left in early September for Florida to attend a Coast Guard Auxillary convention in Orlando before heading to Marco Island. Lee had been an active member of the organization since 1978.

For Christmas that year, Lee, Barbara, and Lee III, who brought his new girlfriend, Alicia Lopez, with him, visited us in Houston. I had commissioned an artist friend to do three identical pen and ink drawings of Maple Point, one for Bob's parents, one for his brother, and one for us. I had each of them matted and framed and gave them to my in-laws as Christmas gifts.

Bob and I did not go to the cottage in 1986 since we had seen Lee and Barbara over the holidays a few months before. But also, soon after we returned from the lake the previous year, our home was invaded by three young men who forced their way inside after Bob opened a knock at the front door. After hearing the commotion, I rushed into the foyer as they pushed Bob onto the stairway landing, holding a gun to his head. All three had guns. I tried to escape but was pulled back inside by one of them and told to get down on the floor. I refused, which seemed to throw my attacker off guard. Eventually, like a miracle, all three men fled from our home. The trauma of this event would stay with us for many years. The only good thing about this experience was that it prompted us to get a dog. We named our beautiful American Eskimo puppy Keiko.

Maple Point on Keuka Lake, Original Photo, Robert Bush Wells. Pen & Ink by Ellen Glass, 1985.

Since the bank Bob worked for in Houston had significant financial problems, and we no longer felt safe in our home, we decided that a change would help us put what had happened behind us. Bob began looking for a new job, so he often had to go out of town for interviews, which made it difficult for us to take a personal vacation. We also did not want to board Keiko or have her crated and put in the belly of an airplane if we flew to the Finger Lakes, so we skipped altogether.

Frank and Joanne had moved to Vancouver, Washington after Grandmother Wells died in the summer of 1984, but came back East each year to visit their children. Frank was vigorously tracing his family's ancestry and had discovered something of interest while researching records in historic Hornby, New York, about twenty-seven miles from Elmira. Frank noted in the cottage guest book that he had become acquainted with Racheal B. Gleason. Bob's Uncle Frank had a habit of being purposely vague. Still, Bob does recall a conversation with his father that Frank had discovered a tie, perhaps from generations ago, between Racheal Gleason and the Wells family. Of course, Lee enjoyed letting Barbara know that her link to Racheal was through marriage, while he was related to one of the first women doctors in the U.S. through blood. I finally determined the connection between the two families from a letter Barbara wrote to her brother in 1980. According to historical records, Aunt Ada was the end of her family's line. However, Frank's research turned up a distant aunt of Aunt Ada's, Ann, who happened to be the first wife of one of Lee's ancestors in New England. Ann did not have any children, so that was as far as the connection went.

When Lee III, Lee IV, and Brenton came to the cottage in July, they also brought Alicia with them. We regretted not seeing her again, but from what we could tell, we felt sure that Lee III was strongly attracted to her. Although it was Alicia's first visit to Maple Point, it was her second time with Lee III's family. Only time would tell the outcome of their romance.

A month after opening the cottage in mid-May of 1987, Lee and Barbara took an Alaskan cruise, similar to the one Aunt Ada and Uncle Bob took about the same time in 1948. Upon their return, they faced the difficult task of saying goodbye to Bonnie, their sixteen-year-old German Shepherd, part Yellow Labrador dog. Bonnie, who had the coloring of a Golden Retriever, was born across the lake, so Lee and Barbara had waited until they were at Keuka before having her put to sleep so she could be buried nearby.

Keiko especially liked sitting in my lap when I was lying in the hammock.

Alicia visited Maple Point with Lee III and the boys for the second time. She remarked that being at such a wonderful place made her feel better about turning thirty-five, and apparently, she was getting along very well with Lee IV and Brenton.

It was September before Bob and I showed up at the lake. Bob had accepted a job with Sovran Bank in Richmond, Virginia, earlier in the year, and I had stayed behind in Houston to take care of selling our home and getting everything ready for the move. It didn't take long for me to feel frustrated about not selling our house, so I decided to store our furniture and join Bob in Richmond. Not long after that, our home sold for less than we owed on the mortgage due to the housing market collapse. We barely had any money to put down on a new home, but we found a small, charming one-and-a-half story that we liked and met our needs. We closed on June 29th and spent all of July and August doing renovations that were needed.

Living in Richmond meant we could drive to the cottage in one day and bring Keiko with us. Our puppy seemed to enjoy herself as much as we did, and she especially liked sitting on my lap when I was lying in the hammock. Maple Point had become a favorite place of mine, and having Keiko, there made it even more so.

While we were at the lake, Lee rebuilt the side doors for the porch and hung them. A Bilco door was also installed in the wine cellar.

A week after we returned to Richmond, Frank and Joanne spent a few days at the lake. They had traveled from Washington state to New York to visit their children on the East Coast.

At the end of September, Lee and Barbara took the auto train to Florida, but this time without Bonnie. They would miss her enormously.

Another family member was lost in 1988; this time, Henry Brooks Bush, the son of Robert and Alma (Jo) Bush, both who preceded him in death. Henry left behind his daughter, Elizabeth; his son, Robert; and his twin sister, Barbara.

This year, when Lee and Barbara returned to Maple Point, they brought along their new Yellow Labrador pup, Maggie, who immediately took to the freedom she had to run across the front lawn without a leash.

In early June, a sudden, strong wind blew down the flagpole. As it fell, it hit the log on the beach, splitting down the middle, causing the guy wires that held it in place to give. The inside of the base had rotted, so it didn't take much for it to give way to the wind. A new twenty-five-foot fiberglass pole that could remain permanently in the ground replaced the old one, which had to be dismantled each year and stored in the basement.

Bob and I spent much of our time at the lake, ensuring Keiko and Maggie stayed out of each other's way. It seemed doubtful that they would ever become friends. Lee and Barbara took us to Pleasant Valley Inn for dinner one evening. The pink Victorian inn is located just outside of Hammondsport and offers gourmet dining in a relaxed setting. It also has four guestrooms. Pleasant Valley Inn remains my favorite of all the places I have ever eaten.

My friends, Kathy and William, and their young son, Christopher, visited in late July. Although initially reluctant, Christopher agreed to go on his first boat ride with Bob and William. Kathy was expecting her second child, so she and I stayed on land, catching up on what had happened the few years since we saw each other and reliving our college days in French class.

Overall, we had a wonderful time at Maple Point that summer. I can't recall ever having anything but a good time at this special place. We missed seeing Lee III and the boys in 1988 since Lee III's company in Tulsa had transferred him to Seattle, Washington. Lee and Barbara took a train to Seattle in late summer to see him and, while they were there, checked out Panorama City, a life care community, which they had looked at following our wedding when they went on their West Coast trip. By December, they had sold their home in Marco Island and moved to Panorama City in Lacey, Washington.

We celebrated my birthday and sixth wedding anniversary in 1989 at Belhurst Castle on Seneca Lake. It was initially the site of a Seneca Indian village and later the Ontario Glass Company. The business closed in 1830 but reopened ten years later. In the 1860s, it was destroyed by fire. The land was divided and sold several times, but eventually, it was purchased in 1885 by Mrs. Carrie Harron of New York City, who began building Belhurst Castle as her private home. Many stories are attached to the castle; some fact, some fiction. Many believed underground passages and secret treasures were hidden underneath this magnificent dwelling. Perhaps even fugitives had hidden there from the law, or it was a haven for illegal gambling and drinking. There were also rumors of hauntings, embezzled funds, and love affairs, including that of Mrs. Harron and her manager, whom she married in 1888 after divorcing her husband.

The beautiful grounds of Belhurst Castle, with its backdrop of Seneca Lake, soon became our favorite photo spot for family get-togethers. But nothing could rival the view of Keuka Lake, whether from the motorboat or the hammock on the porch, where worries die and dreams are born. Keiko loved riding in the boat's stern, sitting in my lap so she could see the passing shoreline. Her dazzling white hair would glisten in the sun, and the wind whipping through the ruff of her neck would tickle my skin. Now that Keiko and Maggie were better acquainted, we could take them on walks together. We also enjoyed having Barbara and Lee join us on our outings.

In May, Lee III and Alicia were married, and shortly after, Brenton moved in with them in Bellevue, Washington. Brenton, age fifteen, came to the lake alone in August that year since Lee IV was in college and unable to accompany his younger brother. Brenton enjoyed skiing and had fun watching Maggie chase ducks. He also mentioned in the guest book that he had enjoyed seeing *Mark Twain: The Musical*, playing in Elmira during the summer.

It was 40 degrees on the porch when Lee and Barbara closed the cottage in late September. They stayed at the Lodge on the Green in Painted Post overnight before setting out for the nearly three thousand miles across the country from Penn Yan to Lacey, Washington. The long drive was worth it, though, since it allowed them to bring Maggie to and from Maple Point.

Maple Point Cottage
1990 – 1997

1990 was one of those years that made me realize that the cottage was more about being with family than just a great place to spend my summer vacation. I especially liked it when all of us were at Maple Point, and the weather was nice.

As far back as 1899, a "Maple Point" sign hung from the dock house facing the water. Bob remembers repainting it when he was in his early teens. At some time, it was stolen. During the warmer winter months, when the cottage was boarded, people would trespass and have picnics on the Point. Most of them gave little thought that they were on private property. Bob and I had a new sign made and brought it with us in 1990. Of course, it did not have the historical significance as the original sign.

Most of the time, Keuka Lake was too cold for me, but this year, it was perfect. Bob gave Keiko her first swimming lesson, and I joined them later. The water was so clear you could see its shell bottom in the shallow parts. Since I had never learned to swim, that's as deep as I dared go anyway. Bob gently pushed Keiko toward me as I stood waist-deep several feet across from him with my arms outstretched to receive her. Lee III stood close by in case things didn't go as planned. I felt proud seeing Keiko swim for the first time, and she seemed to realize that she had done something extraordinary. Still, she never took to the water as Maggie did.

Lee III, Alicia, Bob, and I enjoyed boating, while Lee IV and Brenton preferred skiing. Lee III also spent time rowing the canoe across Keuka Lake and back. One day, all of us except the boys went to Hammondsport. The Village of Hammondsport has a population of less than a thousand and is situated at the South end of Keuka Lake in the Town of

Lee III's canoe on beach near dock house. (Photo by Robert Bush Wells)

Urbana in Steuben County. According to the Village logo, Hammondsport is noted for wine, wings, and water. The first grapes in what eventually became the center of the New York wine industry were planted in 1829 by the Episcopal minister Reverend William Warner Bostwick in the rectory's garden. The Pleasant Valley Wine Company became the first winery in the region and, later on, the first bonded winery in the country.

Favorite activities for those visiting Hammondsport include paddle boating, seaplane rides for touring the village and its surrounding areas, and fishing. The scenery is breathtaking, and several award-winning wineries and breweries are scattered about the region. There are quite a few galleries, artworks, and antique shops to explore, and it's well worth stopping in the Crooked Lake Ice Cream Parlor. I always enjoyed seeing the black Labrador Retriever sitting on the steps of Napa Auto Parts. One summer, we were surprised that a new Lab puppy had replaced the old Lab on the doorstep.

The Glenn H. Curtiss Museum offers exhibits of vintage aircraft, motorcycles, and automobiles. Curtiss, a motorcycle enthusiast, was known as "the fastest man on earth" in the early 1900s, a title which helped put Hammondsport on the map. He was also an aviation pioneer and was deemed the "father of naval aviation." Before the outbreak of World War I, several dirigible and aeronautic outfits set up businesses in the valley just outside Hammondsport, which became known as the "cradle of aviation."

There is also a Finger Lakes Boating Museum with exhibits dating back to the steamship era during the nineteenth century. Another interesting landmark is the gazebo on the village green in the Pulteney Square Historic District. There are frequent concerts at the bandstand, and it's also a favorite place for snapping photos.

After leaving the village, we went to our favorite winery, Bully Hill, which sits on top of a scenic slope overlooking Keuka Lake past rows of grapevines. There's probably never been a similar story to that of Walter S. Taylor, who founded Bully Hill Vineyards in 1970 along with his father, Greyton S. Taylor. Walter was a third-generation winemaker. His grandfather, Walter Stephen Taylor, after whom he was named, founded Taylor Wine Company in Hammondsport in 1880.

Walter was the executive vice president of Taylor Wine Company's Great Western Division, and his father was its CEO. He had always been concerned that harmful chemicals and other ingredients could be found in some wines. He was also sure that most of the New York wineries were adding California grapes to their product, thus; misleading their customers. Walter shared his concerns at a wine event in San Francisco in 1970, hoping to get them to mend their ways. Instead, a month later, Taylor Wine's Board of Directors held a secret meeting when Walter's father was out of town. Walter was fired from his family's company, and on top of that, his wife left him.

Most people who lost everything they had would have difficulty overcoming their circumstances. But not Walter. The small winery he and his father had started as a hobby would become his passion and one day grow into a thriving business. Although Bully Hill was moderately successful, Walter used most of his earnings to pay off debts. His father, Greyton, passed away right before the first vintage was about to be bottled and marketed. Walter bought seventy acres on the outskirts of Hammondsport when he was twenty-seven. The land was first owned by his grandfather and was presumably the site of the original Taylor Wine Company. Walter used the land to experiment with grape varieties and his time to learn about winemaking. His goal was "to produce a 100% New York State wine from French-American grapes developed" at Bully Hill Vineyards. Walter continued to seek reform in the wine industry, especially in his home state, where he had become a folk hero with all his shenanigans that kept him in the spotlight. During this time, Walter, a talented artist, began creating labels for his wines that included the Taylor name multiple times. The history on the back label of his 1976 Seyval Blanc claimed he was the "owner of the Taylor Family Estate" and that Bully Hill was the location of the original Taylor vineyard.

Walter S. Taylor's problems exploded when Coca-Cola acquired Taylor Wine Company in 1977. He lost a court battle with the giant soft drink manufacturer, which excluded him from ever using his family name or claiming to have ever had any connection to Taylor Wine Company. For Walter, this was tantamount to stealing his heritage.

Walter was as proud of the labels he had designed for his wine bottles as his appellations for each wine variety, such as Goat White, Fish Market White, Meat Market Red, or Sweet Walter Red. He was also a fighter who wouldn't let anyone, even Coca-Cola, have the final say, so he gathered two hundred friends and supporters to help him black out the Taylor name on all the wine bottles with a felt-tip marker. As an added touch, Walter came up with a slogan for a new label that featured a goat with a final taunt: "They have my name and my heritage, but they didn't get my goat." Future labels were printed with the Taylor name blacked out, which had become a trademark for Bully Hill wines.

At some point, Walter threw his guitar over his back and hitchhiked across the United States. Wherever he went, he sketched scenes that would end up on a wine label or in the Walter S. Taylor Art Museum on the grounds of Bully Hill Vineyards. In 1990, Walter's van was rear-ended by a truck, and he spent the rest of his life as a quadriplegic from the injuries he sustained in the accident. Although Walter died in 2001, Bully Hill is still alive and thriving.

We spent the day after our trip to Hammondsport doing whatever pleased us—swimming, water tubing, canoeing, skiing, boating, or lying in one of the hammocks. Lunch was on the terrace porch, and afterward, Lee IV and Brenton challenged Lee III and Bob to a game of croquet.

It is estimated that croquet was first played by French peasants as early as the thirteenth century. Shepherd crooks were used for

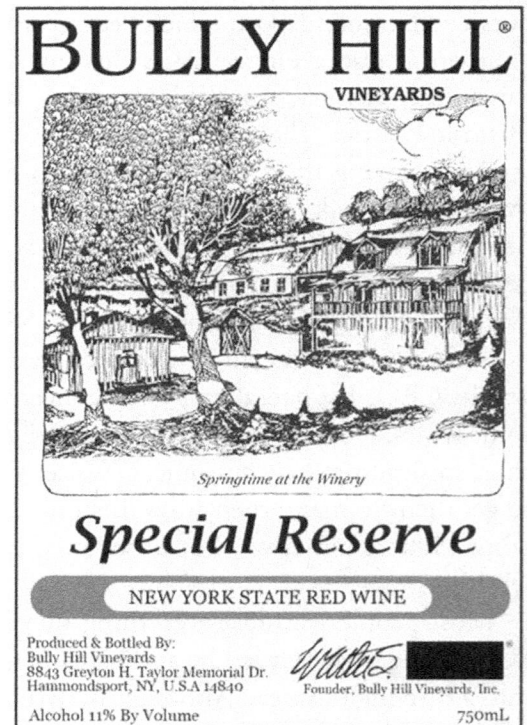

Bully Hill wine label with Walter S. Taylor's name blacked out (lower right)

hitting balls through hoops made from willow branches. The word "croquet" in Old Northern French means "shepherd's crook." A British toy maker who saw the game played in Ireland some time in the seventeenth century is credited with bringing croquet to England. The British elite class, however, were the ones that took to the game with passion.

Croquet is a golf-like game; only the players hit colored wooden balls with a mallet through a course of nine wickets inserted in a grassy lawn chosen as the game's courtyard. The two stakes were set up at opposite ends of the rectangular play area. Game regulations were always observed, but there was also leeway for "house rules" determined by the players.

Often boaters would stop briefly to watch the bustle on Maple Point's bumpy lawn as players shouted gleefully each time they knocked their ball through a wicket. The water carried the voices of those watching us to the end of the Point as if we were doing something unheard of: "Look! They're playing croquet."

One of my favorite parts of the day at Maple Point was breakfast. Barbara and Lee followed the same rules as Aunt Ada and Uncle Bob back in their time. Breakfast was served at eight oclock, and everyone should be dressed for the day—no pajamas or robes were allowed. Lee always had the TV on the news channel while waiting for Barbara to have everything on the table. Alicia and I always helped, especially since we all had different preferences for milk, bread, juice, coffee, and cereal. It wasn't what we ate but being together and sharing stories that made breakfast special.

The news grabbed my attention right before we were seated on August 2nd. Iraq had invaded Kuwait and defeated the Kuwait Armed Forces, who were caught off guard. The President of Iraq, Saddam Hussein, wasted no time declaring Kuwait as the 19th Providence of Iraq. Within hours, the government leaders of Kuwait fled to Saudi Arabia, seeking protection. Iraq had seized control of 20 percent of the global oil supply and could easily access the territory along the Persian Gulf.

This event was particularly concerning for me, having worked for Aramco and traveled to Saudi Arabia on a temporary assignment a few years back. I knew people who lived there who might end up in harm's way. Those at the breakfast table knew what this meant—no doubt there would be a war. There was much discussion that morning, with each of us trying to predict its outcome and how long it would last.

On August 4th, we celebrated my and Alicia's July 28th birthday at Belhurst Castle. It was a beautiful day, and we took photos on the porch before leaving the cottage and then on the grounds of Belhurst after dinner. Everyone had dressed up for the occasion—the older guys wearing coats and ties and the ladies in dresses.

Our time together went too fast. Lee IV was the first to leave. None of us had anticipated how emotional his departure would be. Lee IV had decided to drop out of college and join the army. After boot camp, he was assigned to the Tank Division in Germany. The plans he announced to the family upset Brenton the most, who was still in high school. We were all a little sad, but there was nothing we could do to change Lee IV's mind.

We spent the rest of our time at the cottage, swimming and walking Maggie and Keiko, who seemed to be friendlier with each other when both were on a leash. After we were all gone, Joanne, Frank, Marjorie Lee, and her new husband, Brian Case, dropped by the cottage for lunch. It had been a busy but happy time for Lee and

Barbara. On their way back to Marco Island after closing Maple Point for the winter, they stopped in Richmond for a few days to visit Bob and me. We took them to Monticello, Thomas Jefferson's home in Charlottesville, and then to the Appomattox Court House, where Confederate General Robert E. Lee surrendered his fight in the War Between the States.

Bob and I did not go to the cottage in 1991 since we moved from Richmond to Atlanta, Georgia, in March. Instead, we went to Washington State to see Lee and Barbara's new home in Lacey that year. And since Lee III and Alicia lived near Seattle, we would see them, too. I had never been to the West Coast before, but I instantly liked the gigantic Douglas Fir trees, Mountain Hemlocks, and Cedars. The abundant Rhododendrons were magnificent. Lee always teased me by claiming there were no trees in Texas, where I grew up. East Texas, of course, has plenty of trees, but none are as tall as those in Washington. Lee and Alicia took us boating on Lake Washington in their cabin cruiser. After a while, I felt seasick and had to go below deck. Other than that, it was a nice cruise.

When Lee and Barbara returned to Maple Point that year, they had several projects waiting for them. The old boathouse was torn down, and the dock house floor was painted. The green-slatted rocking chairs on the front porch were refinished.

About a month after they opened the cottage, Uncle Frank and Aunt Joanne visited them from Vancouver, Washington. A few guests came and went in a day, but no other family members could make it that year, including Lee IV, who was now in Germany as an enlisted U.S. Army soldier. Aside from having more time for projects, Lee and Barbara attended Barbara's fiftieth reunion at Hood College in Frederick, Maryland.

Before returning to Marco Island, Lee and Barbara bought a 1992 Buick Roadmaster Wagon in Geneva, New York. It could seat eight people, making it perfect for going out to dinner when several of us were at the cottage.

It was great to be back at Keuka Lake in late June 1992. We missed having Lee III, Alicia, and the boys with us. The weather was beautiful, and we ate dinner with neighbors Ed and Bebe Wellinghoff one night at an Amish restaurant north of Penn Yan. Amish and Mennonite families began buying farmland near Penn Yan around the 1970s after migrating to the Finger Lakes from Lancaster, Pennsylvania. Seeing a horse and buggy tied to a post at the local grocery market was not unusual.

On the Fourth of July, some of the cottagers on Keuka Lake would light flares along the lake's edge. The Thompson boys next door to Maple Point always built a bonfire, and although they monitored it carefully, we always ensured the fire was completely out before going to bed. There were too many tall trees with branches overhead; even a tiny spark could set Maple Point ablaze.

One of the best things about July 4th was knowing Barbara would prepare her potato salad. She would sit on the far end of the kitchen table since there were no countertops and dice the potatoes, green onions, celery, boiled eggs, and other ingredients. Barbara's potato salad was the most requested dish at Maple Point.

My friend Kathy, who lived in Rochester, and her children, Chris and Kelly, spent the day with us. Her husband, William, was in France visiting his family.

Each July 4th since the 1940s, The Penn Yan Flying Club, established in 1939, hosts a Fly-In Breakfast prepared by its members inside one of the airport hangars. This annual event often has nearly a hundred airplanes flying in and serves a hearty pancake breakfast to two thousand-plus hungry pilots and visitors.

Barbara Bush Wells' Potato Salad

4 large red new potatoes
2 hard-boiled eggs
3 to 4 stalks of celery
2 to 4 scallions (green onions)
Several green olives with pimento stuffing
1 small cucumber
Hellmann's Mayonnaise
Salt & Pepper

One Day Ahead:
Boil potatoes with skins on, then place in a covered plastic container and refrigerate overnight.
Boil eggs, then peel and refrigerate overnight.

Next Day:
Remove the entire skin from the potatoes. Discard skins, then dice potatoes into small cubes.
Chop in small pieces: boiled eggs, celery, scallions, olives, and cucumbers.
Mix with potatoes, then season to taste.
Add Hellmann's Mayonaise and mix with a fork (the amount of mayonnaise needed is determined by how well the potatoes absorb it).
Refrigerate at least 2 hours before serving.

We were unhappy to hear that Camp Iroquois, about a mile down the road from Maple Point, was being sold. Fortunately, the purchaser was the New York State Sheriffs' Association, who had rented the camp for the entire season between 1990 and 1992. It was initially used as a YMCA camp as far back as 1921. In 1949, the Elmira YMCA began renting the camp to other organizations to help with funding. The YMCA Board voted not to open Camp Iroquois in 1980 due to low registrations. In 1985, it was reopened after the New York States Sheriffs' Association began renting the camp on a shared basis with the YMCA. Since being purchased in 1992, the New York State Sheriffs' Association has given disadvantaged boys and girls between nine and twelve years old an opportunity to attend summer camp at no cost.

One day a week, the campers would march past Maple Point toward Bluff Point for a picnic. They would sing to and from the bluff, and I always enjoyed hearing their cheerful voices echoing throughout the woods.

I always thought I would like to volunteer at Camp Iroquois if I ever spent the entire summer at the lake. On Friday nights, when the camp was in session, a bonfire was lit, and ghost stories were told. I would love to be a storyteller one day.

Lee III and Alicia came to the lake at the end of August to help Lee and Barbara close the cottage for the season.

July 10, 1993, marked Lee and Barbara's fiftieth wedding anniversary, so they booked a cruise to Norway and the Arctic Circle to celebrate. In late May, they arrived in Penn Yan after a six-day drive from Lacey, Washington, and opened the cottage. Since they would be gone for nearly three weeks, Bob and I invited two couples we had become friends with in Atlanta to spend the week around July 4th at Maple Point. It was the first and only time we had the cottage to ourselves.

Nancy and Mike Henson flew up with us on July 3rd. We rented two cars since there would be six of us. Janis and Paul Beavin could not come until July 5th, so Bob and Mike would drive back to Rochester to meet them at the airport. I couldn't wait to show my friends all the attractions on or near Keuka Lake.

The night before Janis and Paul arrived, we all went down to the end of the Point and sat on the floor of the dock house. We shared some wine as we looked out over the lake and enjoyed listening to the waves lap against the pilings. As the sky darkened, a faint glow rose over the hills across the lake. We watched in awe as a full yellow moon slowly lit the sky like a curtain had been raised. It was the most majestic moon I had ever seen.

While Bob and Mike drove to the airport to pick up Janis and Paul the next day, Nancy and I got everything ready for dinner. I decided we should set the dining table in the living room, so we covered it with a blue and white checkered cloth to go with the Blue Willow and Japanese Phoenix Bird porcelain that had belonged to Aunt Ada and Uncle Bob. I enjoyed using the various dishes stashed away in the tall kitchen cupboards. We even lit candles for the occasion.

Everyone was more interested in relaxing than sightseeing on our first full day together. First, though, we had breakfast at the kitchen table. Everyone was dressed and on time, in the time-honored tradition of Maple Point. Afterward, we headed for the porch, perfect for reading a good book or watching sailboats and other water activities. Bob brought out the telescope that the U.S. Navy had used in World War I, which could be stretched to about three feet for viewing the other side of the lake. I also discovered Aunt Ada's vintage folding reading glasses in the built-in china cabinet on the kitchen's back wall, a novelty we passed from one to another. However, none of us found that holding ornate glasses against our noses significantly improved our vision.

The weather was the only thing that didn't turn out well for our friends' visit. I had bragged about how pleasant it was most of the time, reaching only as high as the seventies. However, 1993 brought record-breaking heat. The cottage was not air-conditioned, so we had to cool ourselves with the few oscillating fans we found in a closet. All the fans in Penn Yan and the surrounding area had quickly sold as the temperature rose above ninety degrees. Although we attempted to play croquet, we ditched the game to go swimming and water tubing. The only other way to beat the heat was to get into our cars and drive somewhere.

We went to the usual places for the rest of the week, such as Hammondsport, Bully Hill Winery, and Garrett Chapel. Another way we dealt with the sweltering heat was to catch a breeze while out in the boat on Keuka Lake, and one evening, we took a moonlight ride across the lake to cool us down.

At the end of the week, we had dinner at Belhurst Castle. It was a pleasure to spend time with friends at Maple Point, and we hope they enjoyed it as much as we did.

Lee and Barbara did not get back from their cruise until after we had returned to Atlanta. Since we could not celebrate their anniversary with them, we decided to have a party in Atlanta for anyone on the East Coast. Likewise, Lee III and Alicia would try to do the same for anyone on the West Coast. The East Coast party took place on July 31, 1993, in our Atlanta home and was smaller than we had expected. The guests who could attend included Bruce Wells, Lee's cousin and his wife Addie, George and Mary Jane Ball, Barbara's Maid of Honor, and a coworker of Lee, Fred Benedict. We also invited our friends Janis, Paul, Nancy, and Mike. After having cocktails in our home, we boarded The New Georgia Railroad Dinner Train. Everyone had a grand time as we dined on prime rib, chicken marsala, and lemon sole stuffed with crab meat. The train followed the tracks to Stone Mountain and back. Following our train ride, we went back to our house for dessert. It was a memorable evening.

A few days later, on August 6, Bob and I celebrated our tenth wedding anniversary by visiting Biltmore Estates in Asheville, North Carolina. There was much to celebrate in 1993.

Lee and Barbara left Maple Point earlier than usual in late August to attend an Organ Extravaganza concert in California. They had recently purchased a small organ for their house in Lacey that both enjoyed listening to and playing.

The first thing Lee and Barbara had on their list of things to do when they arrived at the cottage in 1994 was to have new sod laid on the side yard where beavers had destroyed many small trees. Keeping Maple Point intact was ongoing; hardly a year passed without something needing to be done.

Bob and I showed up on July 8th. We were glad to have Keiko with us again since we couldn't bring her the year before since we had flown instead of driving. Although she and Maggie tolerated each other, one day, while I was lying in the hammock, Maggie walked over to see me, and Keiko quickly pushed her away from me.

During the last few months, Bob had been searching for a new job since he was unhappy with NationsBank, which was formed from the merger of C&S/Sovran and NCNB. He had to travel constantly and did not like his current boss. He had interviewed with Bank One in Columbus, Ohio, and things looked promising. Bob contacted his former boss in Houston, George Grosz, for a reference. Bob was startled when George refused to refer him to Bank One, primarily because he wanted to offer Bob a position at Meridian Bank in Reading, Pennsylvania. George was the President and CEO of Trust, Private Banking, and Mutual Fund Services at Meridian Asset Management Company, a subsidiary of Meridian Bank. Before going to Maple Point, Bob flew to Philadelphia to meet with George who picked him up at the airport and drove him to Reading.

We had only been at the lake a few days when Bob received a phone call from George with the official job offer. Interestingly, Bob had an unexpected encounter with the headhunter involved with his Bank One interview, whose last name was also Wells. As it turned out, they were distant cousins, sharing a family link with their great-great-grandfather, John Wells, who was born in Ohio but died in Oregon, having made his way West traveling on the Oregon Trail.

We celebrated Bob's job offer and Lee and Barbara's fifty-first wedding anniversary at Belhurst Castle. We couldn't wait to move to Reading, and best of all, we would only be a short drive to Keuka Lake. Barbara and Lee planned to visit us in Reading once we were settled in our new home.

It was February 1995 before we sold our house in Atlanta and could buy the stone house we had looked at several times in Shillington, just outside of Reading. By the time we went to the lake, Bob had been with Meridian Bank for almost a year, and we were settled in our new home. It was nice not having to drive that far to the Finger Lakes.

We added another restaurant to our favorite places in or around Hammondsport. Snug Harbor, a charming, two-story wooden structure, faced Keuka Lake's waterfront, with several boat slips and a lovely outdoor dining area.

Aside from us, there was only one other guest at the cottage that year. With fewer guests, more projects could be completed. The weathervane on top of the dock house was replaced, and the roof was repaired in several spots. Lee and Barbara made it to Reading one weekend before returning to Washington.

The dates are unknown regarding the settlement of the driveway encroachment on Maple Point's property, but it is assumed to have occurred between 1995 and 2004. One day in the late 1950s or early 1960s, Uncle Bob, Lee, and young Bob met next-door neighbor Norm Thompson and his bulldoze driver at the top of East Bluff Drive (formerly Bluff Point East Lake Road) where a new driveway adjacent to the gully that ran alongside the garage at the top of the road was about to be dug. Without consulting with Aunt Ada, Uncle Bob agreed to let the Thompsons cut a diagonal path across the upper corner of Maple Point to the property line shared by the Thompsons and the Gleason/Bushes. Aunt Ada was unhappy about this arrangement, so she had legal papers drawn specifying that the agreement would be null and void if any change of ownership due to death, sale, or transfer of property regarding Maple Point or the Thompson cottage. The disputed driveway could have been settled when Maple Point was tendered to Barbara in 1963, but no action was taken, perhaps to maintain a good relationship between neighbors.

After Norm Thompson passed away, Lee and Barbara had their attorney draft a termination letter requesting that the driveway on Maple Point's property be removed. The Thompsons were given until the start of the next season to fulfill this requirement. In some ways, the request signaled that Lee and Barbara would soon have to determine what to do with Maple Point once they could no longer return for the summers. None of us wanted to face this fact.

Bob and I had only lived in Reading a short time when Meridian Bank merged with Corestates in 1996. Bob's office was moved to Philadelphia, which meant we would have to move also. We had decided on West Chester, even though the drive to Philidelphia was thirty-five miles. Most of the time, Bob could take the train, which was much more relaxing than fighting heavy traffic. We had already begun building a house in a new neighborhood and would move to a temporary apartment nearby before long.

It was restful to spend a few days at Maple Point. We tried the restaurant at Bully Hill Wineries, marking it as one of our favorite places to dine in the Hammondsport area. Of course, it was traditional for us to visit Belhurst Castle or Pleasant Valley Inn. We also discovered a new restaurant, Thendara, which was initially built as a home in the early 1900s on the shores of Canandaigua Lake, New York. It was converted into a restaurant in 1957. The Seneca Indians called the place "thendar," which meant "meeting place."

Bob and I decided to explore Elmira while we were at the lake. Our first stop was Woodlawn Cemetery, founded in 1858. A small portion of land was purchased in 1864 by the U.S. government for burying Confederate soldiers who died while serving time at the Elmira Prison Camp during the Civil War. Later on, the Confederate burial grounds became the Woodlawn National Cemetery.

While Woodlawn is the burial place of Samuel Clemens (Mark Twain) and his wife, Olivia, it is also the interment site for Silas and Rachael Gleason. The deed between Reverend Thomas K. Beecher and Silas O. Gleason was signed on October 4, 1882, regarding the sale of Lot 102, Section H. Other members of the Gleason family buried in Section H include Adele A. Gleason, Edward and Henrietta Gleason, and Edith Adele Gleason. Uncle Ada and Uncle Bob were cremated. After Aunt Ada passed away, her ashes were mixed with Uncle Bob's and then buried in Lot 99, Section H of the cemetery, just down the hill from where Mark Twain and his wife's twin monuments are located. There are no headstones to mark the grave sites of the Gleason/Bush families, so their burial spot is a peaceful, park-like setting.

We also found the Brooks Family Vault, where Frances Brooks Bush and her son Gabriel Sayre Bush, Barbara's biological father, are interned. Gabriel was mistakenly listed as Gabriel S. Brooks, but Barbara was able to get his name corrected. Barbara also had the vault sealed, although it had space for four more caskets. The decision was based on the cost of each new internment and the requirement for flat-top coffins to fit in the vault.

After leaving the cemetery, we drove by the house where Aunt Ada and Uncle Bob lived part of the time on Euclid Avenue. Barbara's parents had also lived in a house down the street from them. Both places were in good shape and well-maintained.

Our next stop was the Trinity Episcopal Church, where Lee and Barbara were married, and Barbara, Lee III, and Bob were christened. The church was founded in 1833, and initially, its worship service was held in a schoolhouse where The Park Church now stands. The church building was completed in 1858 and is known for its Gothic Revival architectural style. Trinity's steeple has a tower and a spire, both made of the same brick as the church building. A six-foot gold cross adorns the top of the steeple. There are only eleven churches with steeples made of the same brick in the world, seven of which are in the United States. Trinity is also the only church in New York state with this type of construction.

Our last stop was Arnot Ogden Medical Center, where Bob, his mother, and his brother were born. The hospital was founded through the generous support of Mariana Arnot Ogden in 1888. Its mission was to eliminate factors such as age, sex, color, creed, or nationality when providing care for those living in Elmira or surrounding communities.

For the remainder of our stay at Keuka Lake, we did the usual things that always made us wish we could stay forever. For Keiko, that meant riding in the boat as often as we were willing to accommodate her.

On July 31st, Lee and Barbara boarded a plane to London for a British Isles cruise on the *Cunard Sun*. While they were away, Lee III, Alicia, and their friends from Tulsa, Pat Hoggard, and his companion, whom he called the Lady Janet Comfort, spent a week at Maple Point. Lee and Alicia had not visited the cottage since 1992, so they enjoyed being back and showing their friends what a wonderful place Keuka Lake was. Bob and I were the first visitors at Maple Point, arriving in late June 1997. It was nice being so close to the cottage. We made our usual rounds to Belhurst Castle and Bully Hill Restaurant, but we added the Amish Restaurant, which we had been to before, and The Lincoln Inn, which had opened in 1983. The restaurant was originally a nineteenth-century farmhouse in Canandaigua.

We also took a side trip to Corning, which began as a settlement in 1796. It was initially a lumber town, but later, it was regarded as a railroad town. Eventually, it became known as America's Crystal City. The Corning Glass Museum has more glass art and relics than any other museum in the world and has live glassblowing shows daily.

Bob's cousin Marjorie Lee and her husband Brian visited Lee and Barbara at the end of July. It was a slow year for guests, which may have been why Lee and Barbara closed the cottage early that year.

Once we were back in West Chester, Bob prepared a document for his parents, outlining the facts and options concerning the future disposition of Maple Point. The topic had come up while we were at the cottage in June. Maple Point had been owned by the descendants of the Gleason/Bush family for over a hundred years, with the cost of maintaining the property and annual taxes the main obstacles to keeping it in the family.

Another issue that could impact the final decision was the potential seven-to-eleven-year gap between the time Lee and Barbara could no longer come back to the cottage for the summers and the earliest retirement of Lee III or Bob. If Maple Point were vacant most of the year, the cost and responsibility of ownership would outweigh its limited use of two to four weeks each year. At best, the cottage would remain in the family for one generation since it was not feasible to expect Lee IV or Brenton to take on the burden of owning property that, even now, they rarely were able to visit.

Lee sent a letter to Bob, me, Lee III, and Alicia, asking us to comment on Bob's assessment separately. The final decision, of course, would be made by Lee and Barbara. Lee also reminded everyone how fortunate we were to have spent our summers at Maple Point. If it had not been for Lee's transfer to Syracuse in 1961, Aunt Ada and Uncle Bob would have sold the cottage, thus, negating the notion that passing Maple Point down to the next generation was a family tradition that shouldn't be broken.

I included in my thoughts that I would be willing to stay all summer and assist Lee and Barabara with daily tasks if that would enable them to continue coming to Maple Point each year. They drove three thousand miles back and forth from Lacey to Penn Yan because of their dog, Maggie, whom they did not wish to subject to air travel. My proposal was not a problem so long as we lived in West Chester, just a few hours away.

I had always assumed that one day Bob and I would spend our retirement years the same way Lee and Barbara had. But now, it was probable that the dream would end within the next ten years. I only hoped that when the time came, we could all have the opportunity to select those things from the cottage that had sentimental, historical, artistic, or other value for us. The myrtle I had dug up in June so I could plant it in my flower beds in West Chester would remind me of the beauty of Maple Point when I was not there.

Maple Point Cottage
1998 – 2005

1998 was a new experience for Bob and me, having brought my twelve-year-old great nephew, Ricky Combs, with us to the cottage. Ricky was the only child of my niece Jenny, who was going through some difficult times after her second divorce. Bob and I had invited Ricky to visit us for two weeks the previous year. We toured the Valley Forge National Park, George Washington's winter encampment of 1777-1778, the first day of his trip. The following day we took him to Lancaster to introduce him to the Amish community and, afterward, to the Railroad Museum of Pennsylvania. When we went to Philadelphia, we listened to "Ben Franklin" tell stories, toured the oldest bank in the U.S., enjoyed a horse-drawn carriage tour of Philadelphia, and went on a "The First Philadelphians" walking tour which was being filmed as a documentary. We also took Ricky to Washington, D.C., to explore the Capital, Supreme Court, National Air & Space Museum, numerous memorials and monuments, and The White House.

Ricky's second year staying with us was for six weeks. The first thing on our agenda was New York City, where we toured Ellis Island, the Statue of Liberty, Central Park, and the Metropolitan Museum of Art. The following day we went to the American Museum of Natural History and attended a matinee of *Phantom of the Opera*. During his stay, we also spent a weekend at Hersey, Pennsylvania. On July 3rd, we drove to Keuka Lake to spend a week at the cottage. We had fun roasting marshmallows on the beach and watching the Fourth of July fireworks.

At least one day it rained, so we spent the day on the front porch playing Scrabble or Parcheesi and working the English Inns circular jigsaw puzzle. It was never dull at Maple Point, and Ricky had a blast playing croquet on the lawn, fishing, swimming, and boating. We showed him around the lake, and even though most kids don't like dining in places like Belhurst Castle, he seemed to enjoy it.

One afternoon, Ricky walked to the dock house and sat facing the lake. I decided to join him, but the closer I got, I could tell he was crying. I didn't know what to do at first but decided I should go and sit with him. Ricky was homesick despite everything we had done to keep him busy. I wrapped my arm around him, and the two of us dangled our feet over the dock house steps. We listened to the water slap against the pilings until everything was fine again.

When it was time for us to return to West Chester, Ricky signed the guest book the way a twelve-year-old regards the world around him: "Had a wonderful time and got a taste of the old-fashioned life." We laughed every time we read his words, but we knew there was so much truth in Ricky's assessment. Maple Point was where we came to escape the stress of the modern world. It would be many years before I saw Ricky again, and when I did, it was under tragic circumstances. But the memories of the young boy who stayed with us for two summers have never left my mind.

We missed seeing Marjorie Lee and Brian, the only other visitors who came to the lake that year. They always enjoyed their annual trips to Maple Point. As far as I was concerned, it was the most peaceful place in the world, so it did not surprise me that almost everyone who visited Maple Point felt the same.

1999 marked the end of a decade and a century. Perhaps that's significant enough and makes up for not much happening at Maple Point that year. Keiko was slowing down at age fourteen. She still loved riding in the boat, and even though she and Maggie barely got along, she missed her friend, who was ill and could not make the journey to Maple Point with Lee and Barbara. Without Maggie, they decided to travel by Amtrak instead of driving three thousand miles.

Marjorie Lee and Brian joined us for lunch the day after we arrived. We had missed one another for the past few years, so it was good to catch up on their lives. We also had lunch at Mary Thompson's house next door.

We were expected to help keep Maple Point in good shape each year we visited the lake. Lee and Barbara would assign a task for us to complete, just like Aunt Ada and Uncle Bob did when they owned the cottage. Our project this year was to repair and repaint the windmill and pole that had stood next to the flagpole for many years. Barbara noted that a new American flag was also needed.

Going to the cottage every year was the only constant thing in our lives. It was a haven from a noisy world and a refuge in a world of change. Over the past sixteen years, we lived in five cities. It was difficult to leave friends behind, but the ones who truly mattered would always be in our hearts and minds regardless of where we ended up.

A few months before Barbara and Lee returned to Maple Point in 2000, Maggie was put to sleep due to aggressive cancer. She was twelve years old, and Lee and Barbara did not plan to replace her since they could no longer drive to Maple Point each summer. From then on, they would travel by plane or Amtrack and rent a car once they arrived in Syracuse. They decided to buy a used 1997 Buick Le Sabre to keep at the lake once they were settled that summer.

As suggested at the end of the previous year, a new flag and rope were purchased at Pinckney Hardware in Penn Yan to replace the old ones. It was a tradition that the American flag was raised each morning, lowered each evening, and then appropriately folded into a triangle. When Bob was old enough, it was his job to take care of this. Occasionally, Lee III would do the honors if Bob was not around. This year we enjoyed seeing Marjorie Lee and Brian, who were in the process of moving from Rochester to Canandaigua. My friend, Kathy from Rochester, also visited for the first time in several years.

One evening while we were downstairs watching TV, I heard Keiko's paws clawing at the slippery, wooden stairs, her short gasps of spent breath, and the jingle of her dog tags as she attempted to climb to the second floor. My heart stopped. Not once in her fifteen years had Keiko ever tried such a feat. She would always stand at the foot of the stairs and wait for Bob or me to carry her to bed. Panic-stricken, I immediately ran down the hall, and just as I turned the corner, Keiko's head rose above the top of the stairs. She had two more steps to go. She turned slightly, looking pleased with herself as though she were dancing on a cloud. She must have seen the terror in my eyes, which made her lose confidence; for she began to fall.

I stood helpless as her neck rolled under her and her paws thrashed in the air. My cries startled everyone, but Keiko seemed to understand that the only thing she could do was relax, which allowed her to roll down the steps gently. When her fall ended, she stood up and wagged her tail. Her fall made me realize how quickly and unexpectedly life can end. Second chances always come with limitations. While they allow us to hold onto what we have, they also remind us that nothing lasts forever. It was the same feeling I had about the cottage. Nothing lasts forever.

We had only been home from Maple Point for about a week when Lee notified us that Barabara was in the Soldiers and Sailors Hospital in Penn Yan with what appeared to be a heart condition. The hospital was founded in 1924 to honor residents who served during World War I. Once Barbara was released, I drove back to the lake, bringing Keiko with me since Bob would be at work, and I didn't want to leave her alone all day. Lee and Barbara canceled their plans to return to Washington to give Barbara time to recuperate. All seemed well, so I drove back to West Chester after staying a week to help.

By mid-September, Barbara was back in the hospital for a pacemaker implant. While Barbara was recovering, Jean Bush, the second wife of Barbara's deceased brother, Robert, passed away on September 18th. After his mother was released from Rochester General Hospital, Bob went to Maple Point over a long weekend. I wrote easy recipes for him to prepare meals while there. Keiko and I drove up three days later to take over so Bob could return to work. It was the first time I had ever been to the cottage in autumn. It was cold enough to use the electric baseboard heaters, and the leaves had begun to change colors. It was lovely, and I hoped to come back in the fall at another time and, hopefully, a better one. Lee and Barbara were able to fly back to Washington on October 4th. It wasn't just the leaves that were changing, though; I could feel it all around.

Bob and I arrived at the lake on June 22, 2001 for a two-week stay. June 25th marked Keiko's sixteenth birthday, which we celebrated by taking her on a boat ride. Her age did not synchronize with how beautiful and happy she looked as we skimmed across the water that day. In our hearts, we knew this was her last visit to the lake, and we fretted that she would leave us while we were there. Some nights her breathing was so shallow that we would grab a flashlight and shine it on her until we could detect the gentle rise and fall of her chest.

Uncle Frank, Aunt Joanne, Frank Jr., and his wife, Yone, were visiting Marjorie Lee and Brian while we were at Keuka Lake. Lee, Barbara, Bob, and I met them in Canandaigua at Thendara Restaurant one evening. We had a great time catching up with one another and snapping photos lives that would end up in the voluminous albums we kept. With his bowtie, blue-striped shirt, and black sports jacket, Uncle Frank looked dashing, an image now preserved for future generations who would balk at the idea of following such strict fashion when dining out.

Lee III and Alicia came to the cottage on July 5th. We had not seen them for ten years since they now went to the lake less often and at different times from us. I couldn't help but feel we had all missed something special by not being together and could never reclaim those lost years.

A couple of days later, more guests arrived. We enjoyed lunch on the terrace with Marjorie Lee and Brian on July 7th, followed by a fun afternoon cruising on the lake. One of the things that pleased me was that even when we ate outside, we always used Aunt Ada's Blue Phoenix plates. While some may have thought it was too formal, it was the perfect cottage pattern. The Blue Phoenix was sometimes mixed with the Willow Blue, Flo Blue, and other designs.

Later that evening, Lee IV showed up after a ten-year absence, some due to his time in the army while stationed in Germany. Once he was discharged from the military, he studied art at the School of Art Institute of Chicago. Lee IV had moved to New York City about a year ago, near enough to the cottage to take a bus to get there. He worked for galleries and private art dealers, occasionally designing and doing other art-related jobs. After arriving in Penn Yan, Lee III picked him up and drove him to Maple Point. Lee IV did not receive much of a welcome from Lee and Barbara for some reason that is not known or clear. We had eaten earlier, and no one offered Lee IV anything to eat or drink until I asked if I could fix something for him. Lee IV followed me into the kitchen, where we talked while he ate a ham sandwich. Things were less tense once we joined the others in the family room, and all was well by breakfast the following morning, with the only concern being that each got their preferred coffee, milk, juice, or cereal. We all missed having Brenton with us, but even so, this summer had been one of the most enjoyable times we had ever spent at Keuka Lake.

Once we were all gone, one of Lee's old friends whom he had worked with at Elliott Company, Jim Mahan, and his wife Betty, visited Maple Point. Lee and Jim enjoyed exchanging stories that went back as far as the late 1950s.

All of us, I'm sure, knew that we were speeding directly to the end of something extraordinary. It was like a train that couldn't be stopped, though its whistle was heard incessantly. The only thing we could do was enjoy the ride while it lasted.

Shortly after we arrived at Keuka Lake in 2002, Bob and I decided to explore Watkins Glen State Park, located on the southern shore of Seneca Lake. There are many walking trails in the park, but none are as spectacular as The Gorge Trail, formed when glaciers during the Ice Age deepened the Seneca Valley. This 1.5-mile-long trail follows a stone pathway of 832 stairs that take you along a four-hundred-foot-deep narrow ravine past nineteen waterfalls, high cliffs, stone bridges, and winding streams. The views are breathtaking and well worth the effort to reach the trail's end. The last hundred and eighty stairs to the upper entrance of the park include the stone staircase known as Jacob's Ladder. Fortunately, shuttles were available for the return ride to the starting point rather than having to repeat the 832 steps back down the trail.

Watkins Glen is also known for auto racing and was where the first road race following World War II took place in 1948. Back then, the race course ran through the streets of Watkins Glen, over railroad crossings, residential neighborhoods, and businesses, starting and ending in front of the courthouse in Schuyler County.

Later on, due to safety concerns, races were held at the Watkins Glen International race track, known as "The Glen."

Climbing 832 steps took our minds off the fact that Keiko was no longer with us. On February 9th, we had to put her to sleep. The somber ride to the veterinary clinic had stayed with me these past six months. It was my opinion that, unlike humans, dogs don't seek God or wrestle with who they are. They come into this world knowing how to live, and they understand the meaning of their lives, accepting what is, even their mortality, in the simplest of terms. That, perhaps, is the purest ambition of every soul.

Keiko began to panic when the veterinarian placed her on the examining table. I wanted to call the whole thing off. Bob held her in place, whispering his love, and I sank to my knees beside the table, holding on to her front paws as our eyes met for the last time. It took only five seconds for Keiko to pass. A single tear rolled down her cheek as her eyes closed, and she laid her head on her paws.

I missed our walks and our boat rides. What a wonderful life Keiko had. Now that both Maggie and Keiko were gone, it seemed strange not to have a dog at the lake.

Bob and I also met my friend Kathy for lunch in Pittsford, the oldest village in New York and a suburb of Rochester. The historic Erie Canal, which connects the Great Lakes with New York City, runs through the village. But as charming as this quaint town is, we were more awe-struck by Wegmans, one of America's favorite grocery stores founded in 1916. To give you an idea of how impressive it is, the singer Cher toured Wegmans' superstore in Pittsford late one night and then raved about it at one of her concerts.

On July 4th, Marjorie Lee and Brian made their annual visit to Maple Point. In late August, Uncle Frank and Aunt Joanne moved from Vancouver, Washington, to Canandaigua to be near their daughter and son-in-law. Before leaving for Lacey, Washington, Lee and Barbara had lunch with Frank and Joanne one Sunday.

On a happy note, on September 5th, Lee IV married a woman from Portugal he met in mid-August. Maria João Salema was an established artist who exhibited her work throughout Europe and taught painting at the Academy of Art in Lisbon. She was visiting a friend in New York when she met Lee IV through a mutual acquaintance.

A week after they were married, Maria returned to Portugal for three months to arrange for her move to New York City. Obtaining her green card would prove more difficult, despite marrying an American citizen, than Maria or Lee IV anticipated. Eventually, Bob and I stepped in to help with the process. We found an organization that provided legal assistance in handling her application for becoming a permanent resident. Once that was in place, Maria could teach art if necessary, but she preferred to paint and make art, the same as Lee IV. Recently, Lee IV's artwork was gaining more attention, but it would take time for Maria to become as well-known in the United States as she was in Portugal.

Lee IV was excited about introducing his bride to his family and hoped to do so at Maple Point in the summer of 2003. While some may have questioned his faerie tale courtship and hasty marriage, I had never known Lee IV to be as happy as he now was. I couldn't wait to meet the woman who stole his heart.

2003 was a year of celebration. For twenty years, I spent my summer vacation at Maple Point. As grand as those years were, none compared to this one.

Barbara was still recovering from knee surgery when she and Lee arrived at the cottage in early June. As usual, they took Amtrack, which cut their journey half the time it took to drive from Lacey to Penn Yan.

For several weeks, Lee III, Alicia, Bob, and I had been planning Lee and Barbara's sixtieth wedding anniversary luncheon on July 6th, a few days ahead of their marriage date on July 10, 1943.

The anniversary party was held at noon at the Canandaigua Inn on the Lake. About twenty guests were invited, including their sons, grandsons, and respective wives. Uncle Frank, Aunt Joanne, and their three children and spouses also attended. Old friends and Keuka Lake neighbors celebrated with us: Bebe Wellinghoff, her three daughters, Jean, Ginny, and Sally, their husbands, Mary Thompson, and Fred Benedict, Lee's former co-worker who attended Lee and Barbara's fiftieth-anniversary party in Atlanta. Unfortunately, Alicia could not be with us, but she was truly missed. Barbara's niece and her husband in Atlanta could not make the trip either.

Keiko enjoying a boat ride (age 16). (Photo by Robert Bush Wells)

It was a very festive occasion, and every detail was carefully planned. In true fashion, Uncle Frank had prepared a short speech in honor of Barbara and Lee, teasing them about being distant cousins according to his genealogy research. His son, Peter, gave the blessing, and Bob and Lee III presented a champagne toast jointly. And, of course, a special anniversary cake was served after the meal.

Bob and I arrived on July 2nd, a few days before the party. On July 4th, Uncle Frank, Peter, JoAnn, Frank Jr., and Yone spent the day with us at the cottage. Lee IV and his bride Maria also showed up in time to celebrate Independence Day. We enjoyed being together again, and it was especially delightful to meet Maria. I was glad we had a few days to get to know her before the party. Maria was beautiful and poised, and she seemed relaxed, considering all the people she was encountering at once. Bob and I booked a room at a bed and breakfast in Penn Yan for four nights from July 5th to July 8th once Lee III and Brenton arrived. There were just too many people staying at the cottage, and there was only one bathroom upstairs, where everyone but Lee and Barbara slept.

We stayed in the Merritt Hill Manor, an 1822 country estate. It was atop a hill in Penn Yan overlooking Keuka Lake, but Seneca Lake was visible in the distance. The beautiful house was once a stop on the Underground Railroad. Another advantage to staying at the manor was that we had a gourmet breakfast served without having to do anything but enjoy it. All the work and planning we had done for the party had worn us out, so taking a break for a few days was a good idea. I did miss being at the lake in the evenings when those present would sit on the porch with a glass of wine, occasionally dodging bats as they flew over our heads. The bats had always helped control misquotes, but their numbers had decreased lately.

Lee IV and Maria had been married for less than a year. They were living in Brooklyn, New York, and were looking forward to visiting Maple Point often, perhaps with their children one day. It was a dream we all had, but more and more, a difficult one to fill. Lee IV referred to the cottage as "a very blessed place" in his remarks in the guest book. Maria wrote her full name in the book, in case we ever needed it or were just curious: Maria João Salema Vieira de Castro Teixeira. Maria's grandfather was the governor of Mozambique, Africa, a colony of Portugal, during the time Maria when was born and where she spent her childhood.

Lee IV enjoyed skiing at the lake, and Brenton, who had not visited the cottage for fourteen years, acknowledged that he should come every year. Lee III, Bob, Lee IV, and Brenton played a mean game of croquet on the point while Maria and I watched. We also went to Hammondsport, stopping at several wineries, notably Bully Hill. I can not think of a more enjoyable time than being with family at my favorite place in the world. On our last night at the lake, and after Lee IV and Maria had returned to Brooklyn, Lee III and Brenton took a boat ride across the lake to one of the taverns on the shore. They forgot about the time. It was getting late, and Lee was worried about them and stayed up until they returned. Not much was said that evening, but they got an ear full the following day. Lee made it clear that no matter how old they were, they were under his roof at Maple Point, and he wasn't putting up with any more shenanigans.

Bob and I returned to Maple Point in August for a second visit. We enjoyed having dinner at Pleasant Valley Inn with Lee, Barbara, Uncle Frank, and Aunt Joanne. This time it was our twentieth wedding anniversary that we were celebrating. My friend Kathy also visited us one of the days we were at the lake. The summer could not have been any better.

 Last August, Bob and I adopted a new dog. Halo was an American Eskimo dog like Keiko, but unlike her, he had a troubled soul from being abused the first few months of his life. He was gorgeous, and I was sure he would forget his complicated past with the right amount of love. We did not bring Halo to the lake this year since we were still working on his discipline issues. Initially, we had hoped to adopt two female dogs, but the breeder I spoke to was against it. I had already picked out names for them, Chloé and Angel. I fell in love with Halo at first sight, and even though he was ten months old and had many issues, I knew he was a perfect choice. Ironically, I later learned that Halo's two sisters had been named by their adoptive parents, Chloé and Angel. How enchanted was that? I looked forward to bringing him to the lake next summer.

Lee and Barbara arrived in Syracuse by train and then by car service at Maple Point on May 29, 2004. Their caretaker had already opened the cottage and discovered some water damage caused by an overflow of the gullies during recent rains.

A week later, on June 6th, Lee and Barbara went to Canandaigua Hospital, where Uncle Frank had been admitted after his lungs filled up with fluid due to cancer. It was a sad time. That same day, Lee noted in the guest book that former President Ronald Reagan also passed away from issues related to Alzheimer's disease.

Uncle Frank succumbed to his cancer a few days later, on June 11th. He had worked as a chemical engineer for the Eastman Kodak film laboratory since he graduated from college in 1941. Initially, he was stationed in San Francisco but later transferred to Rochester, New York. Uncle Frank was the family genealogist and had tracked ties to an indentured servant, Edward Doty, and a planter/farmer, Richard Warren, who had sailed on the Mayflower with the pilgrims seeking freedom of religion.

Halo's first visit to the lake, sitting on the porch wearing his red lifejacket, Summer 2004.

Bob and I drove up on June 13th for Uncle Frank's memorial service in Irondoquat, where he and his family had attended church for many years. We would all miss him dearly. I couldn't help but think how grateful I was that just one year ago, so many of us, including Uncle Frank, had enjoyed Lee and Barbara's anniversary party.

Two weeks later, we drove to the lake again, this time with Halo. We had just put our house in West Chester on the market since Bob, who worked for KPMG, was being transferred to Atlanta at his request. We loved living in West Chester, but we were tired of the cold weather, and more often now, I had to check on my parents in Texas.

Halo did not seem interested in swimming, but he enjoyed riding in the boat as much as Keiko. Since we were sure he had never been swimming, we bought him a life jacket. He was so handsome in his bright red with black trim jacket. Barbara noted in the guest book how well Halo was doing. We had been concerned because he was very protective of us, and often he would go after anyone that came near us. I felt sure that having Halo at the lake was comforting for Lee, who probably never expected his younger brother to pass away before him.

In 2005, Bob and I arrived at the lake ahead of Lee and Barbara. We were now living in Atlanta, but we drove to the lake so that we could bring Halo with us. On June 20th, we opened the cottage. Bob could only stay a few days before flying back to Atlanta, but I would remain for several weeks to help with cooking and other tasks that needed attention.

As Lee and Barbara made their way from Lacey to Penn Yan, they talked about their options and the impact they would have on their children and grandchildren. They arrived at Maple Point on July 3rd with many thoughts on their minds. Much of their decisions rested on the opinions Lee III, Alicia, Bob, and I shared with them in 1997 about owning the cottage. No matter how much we loved the place, practicality was a significant factor in deciding its outcome.

Lee and Barbara wasted no time finding a realtor and putting the cottage on the market. We had hoped they would wait until the end of summer, but they were eager to proceed once they had concluded that selling the property was the best solution. Although they arranged a service to handle the cottage contents once Maple Point had a buyer, we could select items we wished to keep.

I was particularly mindful of having realtors and potential buyers look at the cottage since Halo was often aggressive toward strangers. Anytime someone made an appointment, I would take him for a walk, a scenic drive, or park on the road's edge and wait until the lookers were gone. Halo did well around Lee and Barbara because he sensed, I'm sure, they were not afraid of him and would not put up with any negative behavior.

It wasn't easy to enjoy being at the lake, knowing this would be my last summer at Maple Point. I questioned whether Bob and I had made the right decision to give it up. We had only been in the house we built in Atlanta for less than a year. Driving to upstate New York would not be as easy as when we lived in Pennsylvania. But also, Bob was still working, and I would not want to spend the summer at Maple Point alone. The taxes were high, and maintenance was ongoing and expensive. Still, I saw a dream slipping away that could never be reclaimed.

In preparation for Lee III and Alicia's arrival in July, I boarded Halo for a couple of days at a kennel Lee and Barbara had used for Maggie. I thought this would be easier than introducing him to people he didn't know or trust. It was a sweltering summer, and the kennel did not have air conditioning, which only aggravated Halo. When I brought him back to the cottage, I realized I had not made the best choice. Lee was afraid of Halo, and he would stare him down, causing Halo to go after Lee every time he walked past him. It was unsettling for everyone. Alicia had no problems with Halo besides putting up with his bad behavior.

Before Bob returned to Atlanta in early July, Lee and Barbara had, at the request of the home contents buyer, asked us to put a sticky note on any item we were interested in keeping. Any duplicate choices would be worked out between ourselves. Bob and I had started the process since he would not return to the cottage until later in July. Seeing sticky notes on items was upsetting for Lee III and Alicia, perhaps too rude of a reminder that Maple Point was for sale.

Lee IV had wanted to come to the lake once his father and Alicia were there. He was very upset about the cottage being sold and perhaps too young to understand why we could not keep it in the family. Barbara refused to let him visit, adding to Lee IV's frustration. I did not understand her reasoning and did all I could to make her change her mind. Lee IV was crushed, perhaps more than any of us who, at least, got to say goodbye to the place we cherished.

One morning, I was up early and went downstairs to make coffee. I was startled to see Barbara sitting in her chair in the family room, making notes on a yellow legal pad. She had been crying. I had never seen her cry before and didn't know what to say or do, so I went into the kitchen and left her alone. I could only imagine how she must have felt. Maple Point had been part of her life since she was born.

Lee III, Alicia, and I decided we needed an escape from sorting out things we wanted from the cottage. We drove to Hammondsport and then to our last stop at Bully Hill Winery. As we walked back to the parking lot overlooking the lake, Alicia spotted a man who looked familiar. She had recently taken a business trip to Bangalore, India, on behalf of Microsoft, her employer. Alicia and her fellow traveler Tim had met an American businessman, also traveling in India, at the Bangalore Oberoi Hotel gardens. The gentleman getting out of his automobile at the Bully Hill parking lot appeared identical to him, but she dismissed the idea. After all, Alicia lived near Seattle, Washington, and the businessman lived somewhere in the Northeast United States. Although they had met in India, the odds of meeting again in the Finger Lakes region were extremely high. Before we drove off, Alicia pointed the man out to Lee III and me. Despite her protest, we encouraged her to find out if she knew him. Alicia reluctantly went over to the man's car and was astonished to learn that he was the man she had met in India. When she asked what had brought him to Keuka Lake, he explained that while traveling on a British Airways flight, he had noted that the airline's travel magazine featured the beautiful scenic drive of the Finger Lakes wine region and decided to see it for himself. But to think that two people who met overseas and who lived across the country from one another would show up months later at the same place at the same time is incredible.

Bob flew to Rochester on July 22nd and rented a station wagon to load the items from the cottage we wanted to keep. I would follow him back to Atlanta in my SUV, which would also be filled with keepsakes. Since they were traveling by air, Lee III and Alicia would have their items shipped to them, particularly the canoe. Bob and I wanted the wooden rockers with flexible backs and the dropleaf table where the guest book was always kept. We split the dishes we wanted among us, and the other contents were decided on without any arguments.

Another thing that Lee and Barbara requested was for each of us to share our favorite memories in the guest book. Lee and Barbara would stay at the cottage until August 23rd, a month longer than the rest of us. Barbara's last comments in the guest book expressed the difficulty of letting go of the cottage with graciousness and understanding: "It should not be a sad time, but one in which we all had some wonderful times and will take with us many great memories. All of you helped us do this; it was not easy, but well done. May the new owners enjoy Maple Point as much as we did."

Bob, who had spent his first summer at Maple Point six months after he was born, described 1983 as the best summer of all: "when I could share Maple Point with Pat on our honeymoon." He went on to say that "the summer of 2003 was a truly great family gathering" and noted that although the sale of the cottage was "the end of an era, I will always keep Maple Point memories in my heart."

Like Bob, my thoughts centered on my first visit to the cottage in 1983: "I tried to capture the essence of this wonderful place in a poem which I wrote and had framed as a Christmas gift for Lee and Barbara. It hung on a wall at Maple Point for twenty-two years. What was missing in the poem were the things I hadn't yet experienced—croquet on the lawn, breakfast each morning with the family, watching a full moon rise above the hill across the lake, and many happy gatherings with family and friends. Each year I have been here could be another verse filled with its unique imagery, rhythm, and passion." My next favorite summer was in 2003 when we celebrated Lee and Barbara's sixtieth wedding anniversary. This occasion allowed us to get reacquainted with Lee IV and Brenton and to meet Maria. I noted how special it was when Uncle Frank stopped by the cottage that summer and how grateful we all were for having a chance to "stop by" Maple Point one last time. "I love this place. I always will."

Alicia also shared her sentiments about the cottage: "Another special visit to a place near and dear to all our hearts. I have such great memories, from enjoying the company of my in-laws, Lee and Barbara, to watching my husband, Lee III, spend time with his sons, Lee IV and Brent, and his brother Bob and lovely wife, Pat. Not to mention getting to know special friends 'from the lake' and basking in their friendship. Barbara asked that we share our favorite memory here. There are so many—but I will always carry the love I saw here and was honored to be a part of it."

Lee III pondered how any of his visits to Maple Point over the past fifty-nine years could be anything but exceptional: "Every time I came up here was special in new ways—with family, friends, relatives, and events. A hammock, a game of croquet, and a dinner on the terrace were all a part of Maple Point. Where did the years go so quickly?"

We said goodbye to Lee and Barbara and then to Lee III and Alicia as they got in their rental car for the drive to the airport. They were about to pull away when Lee III stopped the engine and got out of the automobile. He walked to the front lawn onto the point, looking out at the beautiful blue waves of Keuka Lake. Lee III then walked over to the flagpole and lowered the flag for the very last time.

Last Look at Maple Point.
(Photo by Robert Bush Wells)

FAMILY TREE OF RACHEL INGALL BROOKS
(November 27, 1820 – March 13, 1905)

PARENTS
Rueben M. Brooks (March 31, 1786 - June 9, 1874)
Married January 18, 1816:
Lucy Muzzy (January 9, 1792 - February 15, 1856)

BROTHER
Rueben Muzzy Brooks (September 4, 1818 - February 25, 1901)
Married July 3, 1844:
Cynthia A. Gleason (April 6, 1820 - July 9, 1906)
  Nephew: Rueben G. Brooks (1849 -1912)
  Niece: Carrie L. Brooks (1851-1950)
  Nephew: Homer O. Brooks (1854 -1916)

BROTHER
John Quincy Brooks (December 18, 1827 - July 22, 1890)
Married February 21, 1850:
Julia A. Locke (March 6, 1827- August 19, 1850)

Married September 30, 1857:
Sarah Filura Vaile (October 1, 1829 - March 18, 1906)
  Nephew: John Vaile Brooks (1859 -1916)
  Nephew: Herbert Hale Brooks (1963 -1944)
  Niece: Julia Zipporah Brooks (1867-1959)
  Niece: Lucy Josephine Brooks (1869 -1925)

SISTER
Lucy Zipporah Brooks (June 24, 1835 - July 4, 1912)
Married September 26, 1872:
Theron A. Wales (July 15, 1842 - September 9, 1914)
  Nephew: Theron Brooks Wales (1873 -1878)
  Nephew: Frederick Theodore Wales (1876 -1898)
  Nephew: Ralph Avery Wales (1878 -1908)
  Niece: Rachel Gleason Wales (1880 -1881)

SIBLINGS WHO DIED IN INFANCY/EARLY CHILDHOOD

BROTHER Rueben M. Brooks (August 31, 1817 - October 31, 1817)
SISTER Lucy Luthera Brooks (September 29, 1823 - March 20, 1827)
SISTER Lucy Zipporah Brooks (February 12, 1829 - April 19, 1829)
BROTHER Name Not Known (November 4, 1831 - November 8, 1831)

Note: it was common practice when a child passed away
to rename the next child of the same gender the deceased child's name.

HUSBAND Married July 3, 1844:
 Silas O. Gleason (November 3, 1818 - April 14, 1899)

CHILDREN Adele A. Gleason (December 24, 1850 - October 7, 1930)
 Edward B. Gleason (November 3, 1855 - May 11, 1940)
 Married May 23, 1877:
 Henrietta Buck (July 4, 1855 - November 19, 1940)

GRANDCHILDREN Edith Adele Gleason (May 28, 1878 - July 14, 1888)
 Ada May Gleason (May 10, 1881 - August 28, 1971)
 Married May 4, 1905:
 Robert Brooks Bush (June 1, 1881 - February 3, 1967)

Most of the information for the Rachel Ingall Brooks family tree was obtained from the family Bible belonging to Rachel's parents, Rueben M. Brooks and Lucy Muzzy Brooks, who married in 1812. The Bible was published in 1824. The family records included births, marriages, and deaths. In addition, these records were compared to grave site records, census records, and any other sources available.

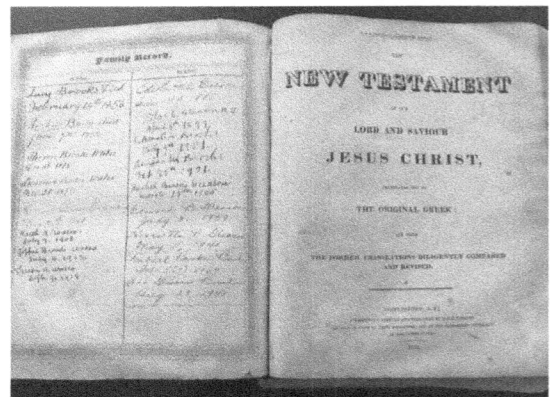

DIRECT DESENDANTS OF GABRIEL SAYRE BUSH

(1883-1918)

PARENTS   John James Bush (1854-1910)
                   Frances Brooks Bush (1857-1928)

SIBLINGS   Robert Brooks Bush (1881-1967)
                   Henry Charles Bush (1887-1975)

CHILDREN   Robert Sayre Bush (1913-1984)
                   Barbara Pauline Bush (1918-2009)

GRANDCHILDREN   Henry Brooks Bush (1943-1988)
                   Barbara Gleason Bush (1943)
                   Lee Arrington Wells III (1946-2023)
                   Robert Bush Wells (1948)

GREAT GRANDCHILDREN   Robert Wade Walter (1969-1991)
                         Lee Arrington Wells IV (1971)
                         Lauren Gleason Walter (1972)
                         Elizabeth Sayre Bush (1974)
                         Brenton Thomas Wells (1974)
                         Robert Charles Bush (1987)

NOTE: Henry Charles Bush adopted the children (Robert & Barbara) of his deceased brother Gabriel, raising them as his own. Although he was their uncle, they referred to him as their father. Henry was also referred to as the grandfather of Robert and Barbara's children rather than their great uncle.

REFERENCES

Keuka Lake, Charles R. Mitchell, © 2002

Penn Yan and Keuka Lake, Charles R. Mitchell, © 1997

Curiosities of the Finger Lakes, Malanie Zimmer, © 2014

"Beautiful Keuka Lake," The Elmira Daily Advertiser, July 26, 1902

"Sign Describes Fascinating History of Bluff Point and Keuka Lake," Bluff Point Association, 6/14/2015

"One Small Step. . ." by Edwin Sayers, Upstate Magazine, June 12, 1988

"My Life," by Lee A. Wells, Jr., © 2013

Brooks Family Bible, © 1824

Maple Point Guest Books 1935 – 1962 (Ada Gleason Bush)

Maple Point Guest Books 1963 – 2005 (Barbara Bush Wells)

Bond – Steven B. Ayres to Homer O. Brooks, Yates County, NY, December 23, 1892

Mortgage – Steven B. Ayres to Homer O. Brooks, Yates County, NY, December 23, 1892

Assignment of Mortage – Homer O. Brooks to Silas O. Gleason, Yates County, NY, January 18, 1893

Deed – Harriet B. Ayres (Abraham Gridley, Referee) to Edward B. Gleason, Yates Co. NY, June 27, 1895

Bill of Sale of Personal Property at Maple Point – Abraham Gridley, Referee to Edward B. Gleason, Yates County, June 27, 1895

Deed – Edward B. Gleason & Henrietta B. Gleason to Ada Gleason Bush, Yates Co., NY, August 1, 1923

Transfer of Deed – Ada Gleason Bush to Barbara Bush Wells, Yates County, NY, August. 2, 1963

"Water Cure is Monument to Gleasons" by Charles Barber, Elmira Sunday Telegram, 1955

"Famous Health Resort Here Came From Very Small Beginnings" Elmira Telegram 1923

"Sanitarium to be Razed," Elmira Star Gazette, July 1959

"Elmira Water Cure," Evelyn Giammichele and Eva Taylor," The Chemung Historical Journal, Vol. 12 NO. 2, Elmira, NY, December 1966

In Memoriam, Rachel Brooks Gleason, 1820 – 1905, by her daughter, Adele A. Gleason

"Elmira History: Taking Gleason's Water Cure" Diane Janowski, Star-Gazette, March 10, 2016

"The Secret History of Eclectic Medicine," www.riverreporter.com, February 17, 2022

"Healing by Special Schools and Methods/Eclectic Medicine" www.budwin.net

"1800s C.E.: Eclectic Physicians + Thomsonian Medicine," www.theherbalacademy.com

Chemung County Historical Center, Branch of the Brooks, Gleason File

History of Chemung County, https://chemung.nygenweb.net/books/1892toc.htm

Herald of Health & Journal of Physical Culture, March 1869 (advertisement)

"Corbett's Electrostatic Machine," Wikipedia

"Electrostatic Therapy and its Use by the Shakers," www.shakermuseum.us.com

"Elmira Water Cure," from Elmira Weekly Gazette Supplement of 1873

"Medical Vibrators for Treatment of Female Hysteria," Rainey Horwitz, 2020

"The History of Vibration Therapy," www.https://sidekicktoo.com

"New Therapeutic Measure--The Electric Light Baths," by J.H. Kellogg, M.D.1898

"A Summer of Hummingbirds," by Christopher Benfey, 2008

"Biography of Jervis Langdon," www.marktwainproject.org

"Rev.(U.S.A.) Thomas Kinnicut Beecher," www.geni.com

"Some Childhood Memories of Mr. & Mrs. Beecher," by Ida Langdon, 1956

"Thomas K. Beecher." www.marktwainstudies.com

"The Beechers Take the Water Cure," www.ctexplored.org

"The Beecher Family and Homeopathy," www.sueyounghistories.com

"Thomas K. Beecher" Park Church, Elmira, NY 1900

"The History of Healthcare in Danville," www.dansvillechamer.com

"Biography of Clara Barton," www.clarabartonmuseum.org

"Washed and Be Healed: The Water Cure Movement and Women's Health," by Susan Cayleff

"Susan Brownell Anthony and Homeopathy," www.sueyounghistories.com

"Olivia Langdon Clemens: Wife to Mark Twain," www.geriwalton.com 2020

"Rachel Brooks Gleason, Pioneer in Women's Healthcare," Kathleen L. Maher, 2017

"Mark Twain in Elmira," Center for Mark Twain Studies, www.marktwainstudies.com

"Henry Kirke Brown: The Father of American Sculpture," www.library.udel.edu

"Steamboats on Keuka Lake," by Richard MacAlpine & Charles Mitchell, 2015

Letters written by Ada Gleason Bush to family on July 9 & 11, 1935, regarding the 1935 Flood

"1935 Deadly Flood Steuben County," The Evening Tribune, July 16, 2021

"The 1935 Flood Devastated our Region," Window on the West Blog, July 8, 2019

"Bush Girl Falls 40 Feet Down Shaft," Elmira Star-Gazette, October 2, 1936

"Distillations/Weather Service," www.sciencehistory.org

"Samuel Langhorne Clemens" by Jervis Langdon, circa 1936

The Press, "Tourist Party from the U.S.," January 22, 1953

"Artifact of the Month/Telescopes & WWI Documents," July 2, 2015, www.acwm.org

www.oldtokyo.com/s-s-president-monroe-american-president-lines-c-1960

USS President Monroe (AP-104), https://en.wikipedia.org/USS-President-Monroe-(AP-104)

"Memorial Chapel on Bluff Point," E. Deming Clark, Finger Lakes Topics, August 12, 1932, Vol. IX-No.19

"Stultz and Bauer: The Tale of Two Piano Makers," Chris Chernobieff, Ezine Articles, October 22, 2015

"Freaky Friday: Silence of the Lamb Funeral Home," Lawyers & Liquor, Boozy Barrister, February 2, 2018

www.belhurst.com/geneva-new-york-castle-belhurst

www.crookedlakereview.com/articles/1_33/10jan1989/10Scherer.html

"They Took My Name, But They Didn't Get My Goat," www.inc.com/magazine/198111201/2124.html

"The Legendary Walter Taylor" by Morton Hochstein, Life in the Finger Lakes, SEP/OCT 2017

"The Battle of the Wine Bottle Labels" by Frank J. Prial, NY Times, August 30, 1977

History of Croquet, www.oakleywoods.com/pages/history-of-croquet

The Croquet Foundation of America, History of Croquet

"The Sheriffs' Summer Camp is one of the Institutes Most Important Activities," www.sheriffsinstute.org

"History of the Sheriff's Camp," Annette Toaspern, Historian, June 2017, www.bluffpoint. Org

"Landmark Thendara Closing to the Public," by Julie Sherwood, Oct. 2007, www.wickedlocal.com

https://en.wikipedia.org/wiki/Trinity_Church_(Elmira,_New_York)#History

"The Story Behind the Founding of Trinity Episcopal Church," Jim Hare, Elmira-Star-Gazette, May 2020

"Have You Ever Climbed the 832 Steps at Watkins Glen SP?" Victoria E. Freile, Democrat & Chronicle, June 8, 2016